CAMPFIRES, KIDS, *and the* OUTDOORS

OUTDOOR LESSONS *for the* REAL WORLD

GEREMY OLSON

Washburn, North Dakota

CAMPFIRES, KIDS, AND THE OUTDOORS
Outdoor Lessons for the Real World
by Geremy Olson

Published by:
241 INK PRODUCTIONS
1113 Sidney Road
Washburn, ND 58577 USA
g241ink@gmail.com
www.241InkProductions.com

Design by: TLC Book Design, *TLCBookDesign.com*
Cover design: Tamara Dever; Interior design: Erin Stark

ISBN: 978-1-7376836-0-5 (paperback)
ISBN: 978-1-7376836-1-2 (e-book)
ISBN: 978-1-7376836-2-9 (audiobook)

Printed in the United States of America.

ACKNOWLEDGMENTS

Thanks to all the mentors in my life
who have gotten me to where I am.

Thanks to everyone at my first NPAA chapel service
and all the friends we've made at the
Minnesota Fishing Challenge.

Thanks to On The Water and Healing Patriots
for providing us the tools to heal as a family.

Thanks to my kids—Daniel, Peter, Andrew, and Morgan—
for being the best guinea pigs a dad could ask for.

And finally, thanks to my wife, Kirsten,
for being the best juggling partner I could have.

*Your relationship with your kids
is the catch that matters most.*

TABLE OF CONTENTS

Part One
BUILDING RELATIONSHIPS

Part Two
TEACHING SKILLS

Part Three
DEMONSTRATING PRINCIPLES

TABLE OF CONTENTS

Part Four
THE FUTURE

*Never underestimate
the power of role models.*

FOREWORD
by Al Lindner

When Geremy told me he was planning to write a book on kids and the outdoors, I thought to myself "that's nice." I've known him and his family for many years now, and I've grown to appreciate how they naturally share time together as a family.

So when Geremy asked me to take a look at the finished manuscript, naturally I said "yeah." I was curious to read it.

I never expected to see what I read.

I've been in the fishing business all my life, and I have never read anything this well done on how to get kids (and adults) involved in fishing and hunting. It's brilliantly done, and I would recommend it to anyone interested in getting more young people involved in the outdoors.

Enjoy!

Al Lindner
Director, Lindner Media Productions

Hard work leads to self-confidence.

INTRODUCTION

Before you read this book, there are a few things I should explain. *Campfires, Kids, and the Outdoors* is a book of stories about the lessons I've learned from my parents along with the successes and mistakes my wife, Kirsten, and I have experienced in raising our own kids. It's a book of examples of the things that have worked and the things that have not worked for us as parents. It is not a "how you should raise your kids" book, nor is it a step-by-step parenting guide. And even though the book is set in the outdoors, the principles I discuss in these pages apply to any of life's activities.

Why did I write this book? That may seem like a simple question, but for me it's not. My second-grade teacher made it very clear to me that I was a stupid, dyslexic kid and shouldn't be in a public school. To get me to want to even try to read, my parents started buying me the *In-Fisherman* magazine. Four decades later, I'm writing for the same people whose articles I read back then as a kid. I guess when my childhood heroes said that a dyslexic kid should write a book, I did. Another reason I wrote this book is to share with parents hope that comes from what I've seen in kids, despite what's going on in our country currently.

When our middle son, Peter, was about to turn sixteen, it was a blast watching him shine doing what he loves: talking fishing. It's hard to believe that, at the time, he had been running Missouri Secrets Tackle with his older brother, Dan, for eight years. At first, Kirsten and I were just parents with a driver's license who took the boys to sport shows. But that year, Peter got his own driver's license, bought himself a truck, and kept Mom and Dad around for moral support.

There's a lot of parental pride in watching Peter and Dan's success in the small little venture they started when they were eight and ten, respectively. But there's a back story that needs to be told, not because of what we see in our boys but because of what we hear from the older generations at these sport shows.

How did Missouri Secrets Tackle come to be? Well, when I got burned in a wildfire as a volunteer firefighter in 2005, we lost everything in a gradual destruction of our business and finances. It was a time when every financial decision we made was a no-win situation. Money wasn't tight; it was nonexistent. Due to our situation—as well as the plan we'd made, before I got hurt, that we were going to raise our kids to work for what they wanted—Kirsten and I started having the kids do odd jobs to earn some spending cash. Keep in mind: Dan was just five and Peter only three at the time.

When Peter was four or five, he wanted to start shooting the .22 rifle. So we asked him if he had any money to buy some rounds. He went to his room and came out with a handful of change and bills. On our next trip to town, we stopped at the sporting goods store. Peter ran to pick out two boxes of .22 cartridges, and we looked at the price to make sure he had enough money to cover the cost.

This wasn't the first time he'd bought something with his own money, but it's the time I remember most vividly. He proudly walked up to the register and placed his rounds on the counter. The clerk rang them up and told him the total. Peter counted out the money and gave it to her. She then took the money and placed it in the till.

Peter's face instantly turned from pride to horrified, confused discombobulation as he looked at me and asked: "What's she doing with my money?"

"Putting it in the register," I replied. "That's her job."

Peter looked back and forth between me and the clerk a few times and then, with a desperate confusion in his young, crackling voice and tears streaming down his face, proclaimed: "I want my money."

Without skipping a beat, the clerk leaned over the counter and, with all the compassion she could possibly muster, looked at Peter and said: "Honey, I feel the same way every time I go shopping."

After a little convincing by me and the clerk, Peter decided to leave his money in the till and take the .22 rounds home.

Fast-forward eleven years. Dan and Peter are selling fishing tackle at sport shows across the Upper Midwest, and one of my favorite things to do is talk to all the folks who are watching them. At one of the very first of these shows, someone made a comment that caught me completely off guard when I heard it. But now that we've been following the boys selling tackle for years, we hear this same comment between five and ten times every show.

What's interesting about the comment is who it comes from. It's typically made by members of the generation that lived through the Great Depression and World War II. These are folks I have a lot of respect for, and they generally don't speak about personal things with much of anybody. That's why I was so caught off guard by the comment in the beginning. And I now realize how close I was to being guilty of the very thing the people are always commenting about.

The conversation typically goes like this: The person asks what exactly is going on with two young boys selling fishing tackle, so I give them a quick little description of how Dan and Peter launched the venture to earn money to support their hunting and fishing habits and to learn the value of a dollar. Then the person looks at me or Kirsten and says: "This is amazing. I ruined my kids."

You can see why this comment surprised us the first few times we heard it. Every time we hear it now, though, we ask: "What do you mean by that?" The answer is typically the same. The person says something to the effect of: "I did everything I could for my kids so that they didn't have to work like I did. And because of that, they have no work ethic, and they expect someone else to do everything for them."

That early show was no different. We had six people stop by the booth and make the comment, and we had the same conversation with each of them.

What's humbling about these continuing conversations is that Kirsten and I probably never would have stuck to our plan of having our kids pay their own way—we at least would not have been as strict as we talked about being before we had kids—if I hadn't been injured in that fire in

2005. And if we hadn't stayed committed to our plan, none of our kids would have learned the valuable lessons about faith and work ethic that we as a family have had the opportunity to learn together over the last twenty-plus years. There's also a really good chance that I would not have gotten the chance to take the stage with Peter at this particular sport show early on and teach a seminar titled "Raising an Angler," where we discussed what it takes from the parent's and the child's perspective to raise a kid to love and respect the outdoors.

So don't be afraid to make your kids work for things. Don't be afraid of not giving them what everybody else has given their kids. What I've learned over the last twenty-plus years is that the most important thing you can give your kids is the one thing only you can give them—and that's you. You can only teach them what you know and help point them in the direction they need to go for the rest of their life. It's a lot of fun to learn—together, as a family—the value of hard work, determination, and what it means to have faith.

What?!
Smiles without technology?

PREFACE

It's only fair to start out with a few disclaimers, so that you can understand what you're getting into when you read this book.

Growing up, I was all boy. One day, when I was three, my dad received a phone call from my mom informing him of my impending death if he didn't come home and find me. I was on a journey to find the whales and sharks that had to be somewhere along the river in the town where we lived—without Mom being on the same side of the river. I knew those creatures had to be somewhere. I'd recently been kicked out of swimming lessons at the YMCA because I couldn't find them in the pool. Really, why would you ever need to know how to float on your back anyway when the fish are under the water?

My grandma told my mom that if I had a farm and a dog, things would go better. So when I was five, we moved to the country. There, I had plenty of room to run free. My favorite pastime was catching mice and gophers out on the prairie. One day, Dad caught me at the back door as I was running in to show Mom my latest prize.

"What do you have there?" Dad asked.

"It's not even a mouse" I replied.

It was then that he explained to me that Mom probably didn't want to see the baby skunk in the living room, and that I should let it go.

I will never forget the patient but stern conversation I had with my dad one night about letting him and Mom know where I was going and when I'd be back. In my defense, I didn't realize how long it would take to chase a bunch of coons five or six miles and then return home in the dark around two or three in the morning. I still can't remember if I got my first watch before or after that incident. What I do know is that my mom lived through raising me, and from what she says the therapy is going well. It's probably important for all of us to realize that grandparents don't spoil their grandkids—they may just be getting even. Just sayin'.

As I grew up, I put all my energy into fishing and hunting. What's interesting is that my dad did neither of the two. What Dad did do was camp and cook. So I grew up camping in North Dakota twelve months out of the year, eating better with meals prepared over an open fire than most people do at home. In high school, Dad and I spent summers together building houses in North Dakota and guiding in the Boundary Waters Canoe Area in northern Minnesota. Looking back on those years, I appreciate the importance of the time Dad spent with me and my sister. Time is one of the paramount foundations of raising kids.

My wife and I had the opportunity to work with a lot of kids before we became parents ourselves. This meant we were "blessed" to witness the causes and effects of parents' actions with their kids, both positive and negative. In many cases, we listened to kids for hours as they poured their hearts out with the frustrations they had with their parents, and/or the things they wished their parents would do differently or better explain to them.

There are a few things we took away from our observations and those conversations.

First, parents that listen without judgment have kids who never stop talking to them. That's right, kids do talk to parents.

Next, kids will always lower themselves to the standards parents set. The lower parents' expectations are for their kids, the less the kids will do to better themselves. The counterbalance to this concept is that parents need to have realistic expectations and rules for their kids. When kids know they're in a no-win situation, they give up just like adults do.

Finally, kids need to know the rules. Punishing kids for something they didn't know was wrong damages the parent/kid relationship deeply. That's why Kirsten and I made the rules simple and the punishments known in advance.

Too many times, kids are punished for simply being kids. Curiosity is what makes being a kid so much fun. Making messes is part of curiosity. Kirsten and I came up with just three punishable offenses: lying, disobedience, and disrespect. We routinely explained these offenses—clearly—and defined their punishments. When the kids did something wrong out of ignorance, we simply explained and then made clear to them that if it happened again, we would apply a known punishment.

When I was a kid, my parents told me I could do anything I wanted as long as I behaved (see the three rules above) and I always let them know where I was going and when I'd be home. Yep, no curfew. What's funny about that is that a couple of years ago, Dad let the cat out of the bag when he told my kids that he and Mom never really knew where I was—because my handwriting was so bad, they couldn't read where I was going or when I'd get back!

Kirsten and I have made plenty of mistakes raising our kids. So another thing we've learned is to never be too proud to ask your kids for forgiveness. Parenting is about growing and learning together with your kids, not being perfect. We aren't supposed to be perfect, so there's no reason to act like it. Keep that in mind as you read this book. The lessons here have been learned by imperfect parents raising imperfect kids.

Having said that: I am a man of deep faith, and the stories and examples in this book are rooted in the Bible. Reading your Bible along with this book will help you gain a better understanding of where I'm coming from and the lessons I'm learning each day.

When all is said and done, this book is the story of how Kirsten and I have learned to raise kids who are self-sufficient, who protect others, and who make wise decisions. It's framed in the context of the outdoors because that's a safe place where families can grow to trust each other and learn lessons that are easily applied to our day-to-day life in the "real world."

As you read this book, then, keep in mind that these are some of the foundations and perspectives I'm writing from. This book is about the stories I can share—and the principles I've learned, along with my family—on the journey called parenting.

part one

BUILDING
RELATIONSHIPS

The first thing to look at is each
kid's ability level vs. their age.

chapter 1

KNOWING YOUR ANGLER

To say that fishing defines me is an understatement. As a preschooler, I was pulled out of swimming lessons because I refused to do anything but try to swim underwater. When asked why I wouldn't attempt to do the back float or swim on the surface, I promptly answered: "There are no fish on the surface." At the age of five, I nearly drowned while swimming at a local lake trying to catch perch with a small net. When Dad asked what happened, I replied: "Well, the fish breathe underwater, so I tried it."

Having grown up a little since then, and now in the process of raising my own four kids in the outdoors, I draw on several principles I learned from my dad that make raising an angler a lot of fun and even more rewarding. What shocks most people is that my dad rarely fished himself—and when he did, he was almost never successful. This chapter is meant to give parents, grandparents, and mentors the tools to raise kids to love and respect the outdoors through positive fishing adventures. You don't need to be a great angler, or even know how to fish at all, to accomplish this feat; Dad is proof. What you do need is the desire and patience to teach and learn with the kids in your life.

Whenever I'm out on the water or in the sporting goods stores, there are a few things I keep seeing over and over again. First, there are young, inquisitive kids who want to look at and touch absolutely everything. Second, I see adults who are so focused on catching fish that they forget how to have fun. Then there are the people who want to catch fish, have fun, and have a story to tell at the end of the day but don't have a clue what they're doing. Finally, there are the poor souls who get dragged to the lake and spend the entire time wishing they were anywhere but there.

Now, if you mix any of these groups together, things tend to go bad. This is important to understand, because most family fishing outings do in fact mix these groups together. If you don't recognize, up front, that this is what *you* are about to do, the trip won't be fun; it will leave wounds. I have friends who hate fishing to this day because they don't understand how fishing groups mix—or, rather, how they don't. Understanding these groups, then, will help you make smart decisions that will leave kids and adults longing for more time in the outdoors.

What makes a kid tick? Well, for starters, kids are full of energy and have a rabid passion to learn. Mix in a little desire to please others, some curiosity, and a hint of selfishness and voila: you have a kid—that is, until adults do everything possible to squeeze these qualities out of them. Whether you believe it or not, every action an adult takes molds the kid who's watching, for good or for bad. It's important to understand that every kid is unique and will react differently. It's our job as adults to listen to and watch each kid to see how they tick, and then act accordingly.

The first thing to look at is each kid's ability level vs. their age. This is essential when you're planning a trip, setting expectations, and picking out equipment. All four of our kids learned to cast a spinning reel in about the same amount of time, but at different ages. Size, muscle structure, and hand-eye coordination are elements you need to look at, before age, when you're making decisions about each hunting and fishing adventure.

Next, you need to watch and understand a kid's attention span. This is not a trick; it's critical.

Raising kids in the outdoors is about relationships.

Many years back, a buddy asked me to help take his son on his first fishing trip. So we picked a nice summer day in June on a relatively quiet lake in southern Minnesota. Everyone was so excited to get out on the water and do some fishing.

We launched the boat, found the perfect bluegill spot, and got some lines in the water. No joke: The ripples were still being created when the bobber was ripped from the surface with a splash. The battle was on, and young Josh had his first fish. This went on for about five fish until, without any warning, Josh put the hook on the eye of the rod, placed the rod in the rod locker, and announced: "I'm done. Let's go home."

Dad had the predictable reaction: "But we got you a rod and a tackle box with all the stuff you wanted, and we drove all the way to the lake and asked Geremy to come with and ... and ... and you're done?"

This story is not unique. It happens all the time, because the attention span of kids is different than that of adults. That's why, when a kid says "I'm done," you need to take a break or quit for the day. The future of the sport relies on it. Kids who were forced to stay out all day fishing and hunting make up a growing group of people who stay at home watching TV because they think fishing is boring.

A learned skill for anyone working with kids is how to stretch them while still having fun. My son Peter and I fished a charity tournament one cold, rainy, miserable April day. The other adult in the boat and I figured that if we could get five fish in, we'd call it good. We knew Peter wouldn't last long in the conditions, so we gave him the job of determining which five fish were big enough to call it quits for the day.

*Kids grow
when they're stretched.*

Well, we started catching fish, and at eleven o'clock we had enough to go weigh in, get dried off, and have a warm meal. We stretched Peter, and I think he stretched us too—because it was cold and miserable.

A couple years later, Peter, his brother Dan, and I were fishing another charity tournament on an equally miserable day in July. At about 9:00 a.m., with not even a bite, Peter asked if we should call it a day, and Dan and I were thinking the same thing. We decided to try one more spot and give it thirty minutes.

Much to our surprise, we started catching fish—lots of them. We took turns reeling them in and netting them, baiting hooks, and bailing the cold rainwater that was filling the boat. We couldn't feel our fingers, and our rain gear was soaked, just like us. A lot of hooting and hollering and more than one hundred walleyes later, we almost missed the three o'clock weigh-in. We all stretched ourselves together and had a lot of fun doing it. Stop while it's fun and you can stretch kids—and yourself—further than you could ever dream.

Now, you did hear me right back there: My boys and I were making noise and fishing. Raising kids in the outdoors is more about relationships than hunting and fishing success. If you do things right, you give kids a reason to use, in public, the outdoor skills they're learning. My wife and I never once said "use your inside voice" and then expressed disappointment when they didn't. We did, however, say "this is a place to practice your hunting voice"—and we then watched the kids compete to see who could whisper the quietest.

One day, I was on the Missouri River with the boys, and we couldn't keep the fish out of the boat. Another boat came zooming up the river and stopped next to us. I asked the gentleman inside how I could help him, and he said: "I heard all the hooting and hollering a mile downriver and came to see what's going on." Peter's reply: "We're catching fish!" Don't let unnecessary rules get in the way of fun. Instead, use outdoor principles to help kids learn why rules matter.

Don't try to be fair. Nothing in nature is fair, and you will waste a lot of time trying to make things fair. Each kid is different, each day ends up different than you planned, and Mother Nature does what she wants. When you try to be fair, you breed resentment—because it pretty much never works. I've found that it's more important to teach this principle: "Put others before yourself." It's a joy watching kids offer the next fish to an adult who hasn't caught one before taking one themselves.

Finally, have fun and learn together. It took me a few years to figure out that I should stop telling Dan and Peter how to fish and instead just have fun learning with them. What I've discovered is that the fish act differently than I thought. I can't tell you all the dumb ideas Peter had that we use all the time now—because the fish agreed with the kid and not the adult.

Spend some time getting to know the kids in your life, meet them where they are, and have some fun learning to fish together.

Enjoy the journey.

chapter 2

TEACHING THE OUTDOORS AT HOME

There are lots of opinions out there about raising kids, some good and some bad. Add in advice on raising kids in the outdoors and those opinions tend to get a little more passion behind them. People love to impose absolutes on kids and treat them all the same. The people who do this are ignoring the fact that kids are all different and come from different backgrounds.

Raising kids is more about concepts than rules. It's about learning to understand your kids and teaching them simple principles that will lead to success. All the concepts in this book are principles we've taught at home and in public to prepare our kids for life—in the outdoors and in the world at large.

As I said before, my wife and I have never uttered the phrase "use your inside voice" to our kids. Now, this isn't because we think our kids should be loud, in the house or in public. Trust me: Three boys can be plenty loud. No, we've offered a different challenge to our kids—"It's time to use your hunting voices"—along with instructions on how to whisper, how to talk with as little air movement as possible to be clear but quiet. The reason it was a challenge is that, if they wanted to go hunting with Dad, the kids had to prove they could be quiet enough to go. With three boys, this challenge was a lot of fun.

Little did I know when we started that boys could get into a wrestling match while whispering at each other about who was the quietest, all while hardly making a noise. The bonus to this twist on quietness is that we've never had to get mad at the kids, because the thought of not going out with Dad was more punishment than we could ever give at home. And if they *weren't* quiet, there was no harm done.

Trust is an important concept to work on at home, and at an early age. What's funny about me writing about trust is that when my oldest boy was in grade school, he routinely told people he trusted everyone but Dad and Grandpa because "they will only get you into trouble." When the boots hit the dirt, however, the kids knew they could trust us as parents, and that we would take care of them in the outdoors.

Trust like this isn't built in the outdoors; it's built at home. You start by allowing your kids to be honest with the questions they have, and by being there for them day in and day out. One of the lies in life is that it's about quality time with your kids. No. It's about *time* with your kids. When you keep your word, listen to them, and don't chew on them for learning, they will trust you. Trust is critical in the outdoors, and it tends to make the teenage years go way better than average.

Absolutes are another thing you can teach at home, where little harm is done. Each of us needs to learn that there are absolutes in life. (Gravity, for example, is one absolute that kids love to test.) If kids don't understand absolutes at home, they can't learn important life lessons with little harm done. We've used every opportunity to show our kids the results of not respecting absolutes. A couple of examples: Asking them to try putting a log back together after splitting it, or to try putting the water back into the bottle after shooting it at the gun range. We all need to learn that there are things we just can't take back.

What Mom doesn't know won't hurt us.

Responsibility is another characteristic that starts at home and makes all the difference in the world in the outdoors. The key to teaching responsibility is to give it and then hold kids to it. Kids need things they are capable of being responsible for. As parents, we need to remember that giving responsibility also means giving permission to fail. If kids can't fail, then they don't have responsibility.

Responsibility also needs to be earned and built upon. As parents, we need to meet kids where they are and work with them to build their responsibility as they grow and mature. Remember: Every kid is different, which means you need to work with every kid on an individual basis. One of the things we've done with our kids is require them to earn the money for the components to load their own ammunition. No money earned = no shooting that trip. It's important to avoid being angry at your kids for failing, and to instead let them live with their failures. That's how we all learn, whether we want to admit it or not.

"Stop" is another important lesson to teach at home. Whether it's with games, contests, or a firm scolding, you need to make sure kids know: When someone says stop, you stop.

Kids also need to be taught that it's okay to *say* "stop." This requires us as adults to respect and listen to them when they see something that isn't right. When "stop" is used by anyone of any age, it's time to talk over the issue at hand and learn together before something bad happens.

I can't express enough how much I appreciate these lessons I was taught at home growing up, and how they have impacted me and my kids over the years. When I was seventeen, for example, my best friend and I paddled a sick guy out of the Boundary Waters Canoe Area in northern Minnesota after dark by counting strokes and navigating with a flashlight and compass. I now get to watch my kids teach others how to fish and hunt year-round—because we've taken the time to teach them the basic principles of the outdoors at home, at the earliest ages we could.

Don't forget, it's okay to have fun ... really.

HAVING FUN

Many of you are reading this book because, like me, you have an internal, unquenchable longing to be in the outdoors. Others of you are reading this book because you're looking for information on how to participate in outdoor activities for the first time, or you want to learn how to be more successful in your outdoor adventures.

This chapter is going to be a little different from the rest because it's about what we, as adults, *need to learn from the kids* we take into the outdoors.

In a nutshell: We need to learn how to have fun again.

I was the kid who loved to fish. We lived on the river in my hometown, and I could explore the banks and catch bullheads all day long. It's like the old proverb says: "Give a man a fish, you feed him for a day; teach a man to fish and all his money will go to fishing for the rest of his life." Yes, I love to fish, and I don't apologize for it. I did, however, have some experiences growing up that really made me wonder. In fact, quite frankly, they're the reason I've written this book.

I'll never forget the first time someone other than my dad took me fishing. It took two to three hours to get everything put together, get to the lake, and try to fish. These two guys could barely run the boat, they had no plan, and they argued about everything. During this exercise in futility, one of them stepped on the other's new rod and the swearing went into overdrive. The broken rod tip turned into a rod getting broken over the owner's knee and promptly being thrown into the lake.

Needless to say, I did not have fun that day.

I'm telling you this story for one reason: It isn't all that hard to make a trip fun. These two guys were just a worst-case scenario of what *not* to do: lose perspective.

This is where kids have a leg up on us adults; they look to have fun in almost everything they do. Fun involves a few things: risk, adventure, companionship, and learning your limits, just to get started. Many of us adults were taught that these concepts are bad for kids to experience, and thus concepts we need to avoid. As a result, we have generations of kids who can only experience them on a video game console. For more than thirty years now, I have been actively involved with kids in the outdoors. When you let them have fun and show them how, I promise you: They will be hooked for life.

Jay was the guy in my life who took the time to teach me how to fish and hunt. My dad taught me how to live in the outdoors. We camped twelve months a year in North Dakota, cooking better over an open fire than most people eat at home. Jay was the guy who took me out and taught me not only how to hunt and fish, but also how to have fun doing it. I never knew it at the time, but Jay and my dad instilled principles in me that made it possible for me to raise my own kids in the outdoors.

Jay, for example, never took the same road twice. I had so much fun exploring new areas of our state. As we drove, the two of us talked about each local area's history, and how we would hunt in that area if we ever had the chance.

I hope the statute of limitations is up on Jay teaching a minor how to gamble, but anyway ... we had an ongoing bet of a dime for the first fish and a quarter for the biggest fish every trip. We fished in the cold, the rain, the wind, and the heat. We talked and told stories, in the boat and onshore, having fun through it all. I never saw him get mad, even when the front wheel fell off the truck during a trip to the middle of nowhere—and long before cell phones existed. To this day, I never fish without a dime and quarter in my tackle box, in honor of what I learned about fishing and life from Jay.

I remember when I took my own kids to a little fishing pond for the first time. I was doing my best to teach them how to fish: showing them how to cast, how to hold the rod, how to set the hook, and all the other fundamentals I thought they needed to know. But at four and two years old, they weren't getting it—and I started to get stressed. That's when I began to ask myself: *"What am I doing wrong? What should I be doing differently? What if they don't get it? What if they don't catch any fish?"* In hindsight, all they wanted to do was dangle a hook in front of the dock with these little gills that were only two or three inches long.

It was then that the right question hit me: *"Do I want to be like the first two guys who took me fishing, or like Jay?"* Yeah, it was a no-brainer question, but the answer changes your perspective profoundly. I needed to let the kids have fun, which meant discovering and exploring. So we pulled out smaller hooks and played on our bellies with tiny bluegills for hours.

Some of my best memories with my kids involve shore fishing for cats and carp or hitting the water for drum and goldeye in the boat. I will never pass up the opportunity when the kids ask to learn something new. One year, we worked on *Deadliest Catch* North Dakota crawfishing, tournament bass fishing 101, and Dad riding in the front of the boat with a cup of coffee. Lots of things went wrong, but they always do. It's our job as adults to learn with the kids in the outdoors, stretch them, and have fun doing it. If, for example, you're out fishing and your targeted fish isn't biting and all you're catching are white bass, go white bass fishing.

Don't let great expectations ruin a fun day on the water.

Each year, we get to go to Gull Lake, near Brainerd, for the Minnesota Fishing Challenge. The kids started out having more fun releasing fish at the tournament than I think the anglers did catching the fish. The event is three days of untethered, laugh-till-you-hurt rock bass fishing. That's right, rock bass fishing. It's not about the fish; it's about the fun. Today, the kids help sponsor and raise money for the tournament—and they still fish in it too.

The reality is pretty simple: As adults, we need to give kids the opportunity to have fun in the outdoors. This means letting them explore with other people, teaching them what we know, and learning how to take calculated risks together.

We also need to learn how to put life in perspective, enjoy the company of who we're with, and be content with what nature gives us on a particular day. In the outdoors, expectations only ruin the learning process; you need to have fun with the conditions that Mother Nature provides each day.

Taking kids fishing is really hard to screw up if you remember the goal: It's about having a positive outdoor experience. If you let yourself and the kids you're with have fun, you're over halfway there.

Small-pike lakes are a great classroom.

LEARNING TOGETHER

A couple years ago, I had the opportunity to watch my son Peter teach a seminar to high school students. It was called "The Science of Fishing," and in it, Peter talked about the importance of understanding the scientific method in designing fishing tackle.

Sounds pretty complicated when you first think about it, but in reality, it's the part of fishing I love the most. When you boil it down, all Peter was talking about is how we as a family learn together. The best way I can think of to describe what I'm talking about is to share some stories that our family has lived over the last twenty-plus years—along with a few I can't tell you the conclusion to because we're still experiencing them together.

One of the most feared events in many an elementary school parent's year is the science fair. With my son Dan, though, it meant another reason for the two of us to go fishing.

Those of you who have been at angling for a number of years: I am willing to bet that you have some opinions you are pretty set in. I have one friend, for example, who likes to say that "walleye will bite any color as long as it's chartreuse." Well ... Dan was watching a show talking about how you need to have red hooks to catch walleye. He looked at me and asked: "Dad, how do they know that?" So I talked to him about how people try different things and stick with the things that work.

*The kitchen is a top-secret lab...
Shhhh, don't tell Mom.*

The next week, Dan came home with his science fair paperwork and declared: "I want to figure out if walleye like red." So we spent the next month figuring out how to color a minnow so that it could still live to swim in an aquarium. What we learned was that every available coloring option in the catalogs wouldn't kill a minnow but would paralyze it.

So we began testing every method we could think of to color a minnow. For starters, we learned all sorts of ways that will—for lack of better words—not keep you in the good graces of the wife. Let's just say it's not a good idea to try food coloring on a white countertop with flopping minnows.

The science fair project was a lot of fun, and its outcome produced fishing discoveries we use to this day. Turns out that Sharpie markers are the best way to color a minnow. Dan put a green, a yellow, a blue, and a red minnow—along with a minnow with no color—into the tank, and the walleye ate an equal number of each of the colored minnows first and second ... and the plain minnow third. Today we carry Sharpies in our boat to color everything from minnows and plastics to spinners.

On the grosser side of learning together: We have always looked at what's inside the stomachs of the fish we clean. For the most part, it's just status quo. But every once in a while, you find something that makes you scratch your head. Case in point: We cleaned pike one day after ice fishing on our favorite Christmas Day lake and found some perch in the bellies of the pike. Now, that isn't uncommon—except, in this case, for the *size* of the perch. Out of two limits of pike, the smallest perch was nine inches long and the biggest pike was six pounds.

On another ice fishing trip, we were cleaning walleyes and found that some of them had frogs in their stomachs while others had only fatheads and perch. We couldn't figure it out, so we picked up an underwater camera and started taking note of what we caught. The first thing that surprised me was seeing frogs swimming around on the bottom of the lake during the winter. I was always taught that frogs hibernate in the mud all winter. But there they were, swimming around, ready to become a walleye meal.

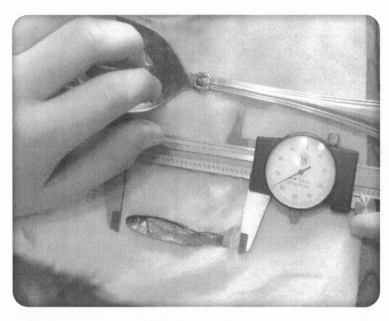

Reloading tools ✓
Minnows ✓
Aquarium ✓
Now for the science fair!

One day, the boys decided to see how many fish we caught on a one-minnow rig vs. a two-minnow rig. We set up two buckets to keep track of the fish we brought in on each of the setups. At the end of the night, it seemed pretty equal and not a big deal. But for whatever reason, we kept the fish separate until we cleaned them when we got home.

To our surprise, all the fish we'd caught on the rigs with one minnow had perch and fathead minnows in their bellies. All the fish we'd caught on the two-minnow rigs were full of frogs and had no minnows in them. Who would've thought?

Over the last couple of years, a tackle company has given us some lures to product-test for them. When we asked how they worked, the answer was: "See what you come up with." At first, that response was a little annoying. But as we started fishing with the lures, we realized how much fun it was to figure out how to use them. Come to find out we were pioneering new ways to fish the lure that even the company hadn't thought of. None of this knowledge would have been possible without our willingness to learn together in a fun and exciting way.

Simple experiments like these are easy to do and make fishing fun. I know that, as a lifelong angler, I have learned more from learning with my kids than I ever would have on my own.

The added benefits are even better. Learning the outdoors together helps you and your kids communicate more effectively. It puts life into perspective and helps us as parents better understand how our kids learn—which, in turn, helps us be better advocates for them when necessary. Not to mention that fishing, when you do it together, is way more fun than any video game or social media site.

I challenge you to find some fun opportunities to learn together with kids, yours or others'. The relationships you build with your young anglers will be lifelong—and worth every minute.

*Don't be afraid to be persistent
until you find someone to help.*

WHO TO ASK

Picking the right lake to fish can be tough even on a good day—even if you know how to fish.

If you're *learning* how to fish and how to take a kid fishing, the challenge can seem even more daunting. Add in not knowing who to ask for advice and information and suddenly it feels impossible to find a lake with fish that are biting, or to figure out what to use to catch them.

I'll never forget the first time my dad took me ice fishing. He did what most parents do when their seven-year-old son hounds them to take them fishing and they have no idea what to do: He borrowed Grandpa's old chipping bar and we went to the place he knew best—yep, the lake we went swimming in all the time.

He took me to the spot where he remembered me catching fish all summer, and we started to chip. After an eternity of working on this cold, late-winter day, we hit the sand bar I had fished on all summer.

We didn't catch a single fish that day.

In hindsight, I'm pretty sure Dad ended up more frustrated than I did, because even though he didn't fish himself, he liked being successful just as much as the next guy.

To top things off, he didn't know who to ask or where to look for the right information. Real-time, solid information is vital to catching fish and having a good trip. But knowing where to get it can be as hard as finding a four-millimeter bead in your living room carpet.

You have lots of options, though.

First, there are web forums that are full of *partial* information. You get lakes, depths, colors, and sometimes specific lures. As a rule, however, you need to realize that these forums are always leaving something out. They're like a puzzle that's missing two or three pieces. Don't be afraid to ask questions on these forums; just realize that you're getting only *part* of the story. Be up-front about your ability level and the fact that you're looking for a place to take kids fishing. It may take a few tries, but typically somebody will chime in with some practical information and ideas that generally help.

The second place you can look for good information is with your state's fisheries professionals. Some of my favorite fishing trips with groups of kids have unfolded after chats with the local fisheries biologist about some low-pressure hotspots. Look on your state's fisheries website for outreach and fishing days. These are great opportunities to learn, and to meet the people who are glad to help you catch fish. (You're going to hear me repeat this a lot.) Make sure you take the time to say thank you. One of the best ways to do so is to simply send a picture of your successful day. It's always uplifting for fisheries professionals to hear—and see—that you caught fish because of their help.

Professional anglers are another overlooked option. It's their job to be out on the water and staying in touch with the fish. They also have a responsibility to share information and teach others how to fish. Any respectable pro will help you out the best they can.

Don't forget to take a picture to share with the people who helped.

Your best bet is to look for the pros in the area you're looking to fish. Remember one thing, though: Whenever you're getting information from anyone—but even more so with the pros—be honest about your questions and don't misuse the information. I say this because one time, we helped a guy with information he claimed he'd use to take some new anglers fishing—only to find out later that he was actually using it to fish a tournament. So make sure you use the information you're given for the purpose you stated.

The one exception to asking a pro for information involves guides. If they *offer* you something, it's okay to take it. But, for ethical reasons, I would stay away from *asking* guides for information. Their livelihood is taking people out fishing and teaching them how to catch fish. So if you want to go that route, hire them. With a good guide, you'll learn more about how to catch fish in a day than you may in years on your own. If you can afford it, it's worth it.

Again, don't forget to say thanks when the information you get from a pro is helpful. All pros need to provide their employers/sponsors with reports showing they're doing their job. So help them out with a picture and a thank-you note after your successful trip.

Your local bait shop is another great source of information. When I'm talking about local bait shops, I mean the ones run by fishermen—not just a gas station with some tackle. Local bait shop staff know what, where, and why the fish are biting. My son Peter and I stopped in for bait at one of our favorite shops the other day and left an hour later with some great information for a tough bite we were experiencing.

Just as you do for guides, you need to support your local bait shops. Whenever possible, buy what you can from them; it keeps them in business. You can find a lot of cheap stuff at box stores and online, but none of it comes with the valuable insights your local bait shop can give you.

Be sure, too, that whenever possible, you stop back at the bait shop after your fishing day is over and share how it went. The essence of a good local bait shop is the relationship that anglers and owners have and the mutual sharing of information. And again: Don't forget to say thank you!

Finally, remember friends and family: Make sure you ask around amongst the people you already know. They may not have the insight you need, but almost everyone knows someone who knows how to fish.

The year after my first ice fishing experience, Dad asked around and his uncle invited us to go to a small perch lake some of the locals knew about. I got to experience three hours of one-fish-after-another. It may not have been a good thing for Dad, because that was the day I got hooked on ice fishing! But it was a day we'll never forget because it was a positive outdoor experience. And it happened because Dad asked around until someone helped. So don't give up if you don't find the information you need on the first few tries.

Some of you are reading this because you have no idea where to go fishing yourself, much less where you'd take someone else out to catch fish. Others of you are getting the hang of fishing but aren't confident taking others out. Still others of you have a hard time *not* catching fish wherever and whenever you go.

No matter where you fall on the spectrum of fishing experience and expertise, take the time to build relationships with others. There are lots of people out there who want to learn how to fish and are looking for someone to teach them. If you're that person, don't be afraid to ask until you find help. If, on the other hand, you know how to fish, don't wait to make the newcomers ask. Find them and help them out.

Relationships are built onshore,
with sticky marshmallows to hold them together.

SHORE FISHING FUN

What pops into your head when someone says "let's go fishing"? What appears in your cartoon bubble of what the trip will look like?

For many, the picture features a boat, lots of tackle and rods, and the hope of a fish picture worthy of a magazine cover. For others, it's the image of a passel of folks on a pontoon, with stuff everywhere and maybe the hope of *some* fish.

I'd like to give you another image to consider—an image that fits perfectly with raising kids and building relationships.

Looking back on all the fishing adventures I've had with my kids over the last twenty-plus years, the most memorable, meaningful, and fun trips have all involved shore fishing. Yep, shore fishing.

Don't get me wrong: Fishing in a boat is fun. But it comes with limitations and experiences that aren't present when you're shore fishing. (These limitations and experiences aren't *bad*; like I said, they're just *present*.) So let's talk about some shore fishing fun.

Over the years, I've fished from Georgia to Montana, so I understand that shore fishing tactics are different wherever you go. To be clear, though, this isn't a *fishing* tactic chapter anyway; it's a *parenting* tactic chapter.

I grew up shore fishing because our family had neither the disposable income nor the desire to buy a boat with a motor. What we did have was a nice little lake fifteen minutes from home that we visited sometimes three or four times a week during the hot summer. What sticks out in my mind about my many days at this lake is that we could swim, fish, grill, or have a campfire and there was something for everyone to do together as a family.

Fast-forward a bunch of years and my wife and I had two small children, living with them in southern Minnesota near multiple lakes where we could take them shore fishing and play in the water. Keep fast-forwarding to today in North Dakota, and our family still enjoys hanging out onshore, having fun and even fishing together.

When it comes to shore fishing with your family, there's a handful of tactics that will help you make the experience fun and memorable.

First, don't put a ton of money into tackle and other equipment. At most of the places we fish, for example, you can get by with simple bottom rigs or bobber setups. And almost every rod holder we've ever used is homemade.

Why am I bringing this up? Well, as a parent, the more money you put into something, the easier it is to get angry when it gets broken. I'm not saying that you shouldn't teach your kids to take care of things. But when you don't have a lot of money invested as a parent, you have the freedom to not worry as much. One of the most expensive and valuable pieces of equipment we've used when shore fishing over the last twenty years is a twenty-dollar barbecue grill that we bring along when we can't have campfires.

Remember: Kids don't care how much money you spend on them. What they care about is spending time together. So when you focus on having fun and learning together, you remove a lot of the stress that parents too often inflict on themselves.

Next tip: Shore fishing allows everyone the room and freedom to do something different—so let it happen. One kid can throw rocks, one kid can swim, one can chase frogs, and one can pick their nose with the grass they found on the shoreline—all while waiting for a fish to bite. In other words, it's hard for people to get bored if they all have something to do.

I have to put in a disclaimer here, though: I get in a lot of trouble with my wife when we go shore fishing, because moms inherently have rules for kids that are appropriate for the house but not for the shoreline. This is the place to get dirty, kiss frogs, throw snakes, and get your shoes wet. Wait a minute ... why are they wearing shoes?

If you haven't figured it out yet, food is also an extremely important part of this equation. Remember this principle: "Never get cold, never get hungry." Make sure you have plenty of snacks, and spring for the really expensive hotdogs sometimes—because, again, if a kid drops one in the fire, it's something to laugh about, not get angry about. In the spring and fall, cooking over an open fire is a fun thing to do while you're waiting for the fish to bite. And ending the night with blueberry or peach cobbler is a bonus. Don't worry about dishes and balanced meals; this is a time to relax and have fun together.

Here's another clever parenting tactic that is worth every minute: Whenever the opportunity presents itself, bypass bedtimes and normal evening rituals for the investment in stories that build relationships. One fall night, when all the kids had school the next day and the walleye bite wasn't fast and furious, we had started to pack up to go home when we realized that the stars were exceptionally bright on a cold, crisp night. So we put out the campfire and all six of us lay on the ground, watching the stars much longer than we had ever planned. Yes, the kids were crabby the next morning, but in the long run it was worth every minute.

On another occasion, we had an epic bite and lost track of how many fish we caught after fifty. So we fished until we ran out of bait and were all too tired to stay out any longer. What's important to remember about this night is that the biggest walleye was maybe thirteen inches long. But the memories were keepers.

In the old days, the rule was no radios. Nowadays we just say no technology, because there's no sense being outside around a fire on the shoreline if you allow something to get in the way of people talking to each other. And when I say "talking to each other," I mean half storytelling and 75 percent picking on the kids.

Another disclaimer: As a rule, dads are horrible at taking something seriously and getting angry. I'm sure those emotions are still appropriate in the car while you're on vacation, but they are not acceptable when you're shore fishing.

Shore fishing puts you in an environment where memories are easily made if you simply let them happen. You cannot plan positive, lifelong memories. Most of the memorable shore fishing trips our family has taken over the years have been last-minute decisions made by my wife and me because the weather was right, we all needed a break, and it just made sense.

So save some money, eat some cheap food over a campfire, stay out too late, laugh together, and make memories on a shoreline near you.

You can't do it perfectly, but you can do it together.

DOING IT TOGETHER

I didn't grow up in a poor family. But I didn't grow up in a family that could just go to the sporting goods store and buy whatever we wanted, either. If we wanted something, we needed to plan, prioritize, and save to get it.

This is the situation for many of us outdoor-minded families today. Sure, we can go to the local store or online and drop a *credit card number* to get what we want. But that just misses the point.

Living in the outdoors is about responsibility, conservation, self-sufficiency, stretching ourselves, and so much more. Raising kids in the outdoors is about helping them learn all the things the outdoors can teach them while we're still learning those lessons ourselves.

What's important is that we do it together. Picking out an adventure, figuring out what it takes to make it happen, living the journey together, telling the stories of what we've learned along the way—all of it is amazing and goes against conventional thinking. Families that fish together fish, families that shoot together shoot, families that camp together camp, families that boat together boat, and so on.

You may still find it hard to believe that I grew up in a home that didn't hunt or fish. In fact, my dad was the guy who got skunked when everyone else in the fishing boat caught their limit. What Dad did know, though, was how to camp and cook. This is important to understand, because when we choose to do things together as a family, we, as parents, need to consciously decide to sacrifice some of what we want so that we can help others learn. In my case, the older I got growing up, the more our camping trips revolved around hunting and fishing. But it wasn't because Dad wanted to go hunting and fishing. It was because he

*Skip tee time
and set up a tree time.*

sacrificed what he wanted and knew how to do to help me develop my outdoor skills.

My whole life, I wanted to learn how to shoot archery but just never had the resources. So one summer, when my two oldest boys started getting the itch to shoot, we went through the process of researching bows together, earning the money we needed, and then buying three bows. As we shot and learned together, we laughed a lot, winced in pain with every string slap, and competed to become good enough to get in a tree stand and get a deer.

Seven years later, all six of us in the house had our own bow, and we loved playing a game or two of archery darts in the backyard while the food was on the fire for supper. The only difficulty then was going to be filling that many archery tags in the fall. Trust me: With four teenagers, we needed the meat in the freezer!

The following summer, we had all sorts of things on the agenda. My youngest was in the process of figuring out what rifle she wanted to get for the next year's deer season, one of the boys was determined to learn how to kayak, and his older brother was learning what it took to get the big boat out on the water by himself. As a family, we got to coach and laugh with (and at) each other along the way as we learned everything together.

All of what I'm describing takes patience and some grace, to be sure, but it's worth it. I am definitely a better outdoorsman because of what I've learned being in the outdoors with my family. The kids' curiosity and questions help us as adults to realize what we *truly* know compared to what we think (or thought!) we know.

*The most effective way to show
our kids we love them and care
for them is to give them our
time and attention.*

Additionally, when we set aside the time and our own passions to invest in our kids, we show them that we care. This cultivates healthy relationships where communication and trust exist. And you need communication and trust to build a solid foundation and relationship with your kids. The result will be kids who are eager to learn and explore instead of sitting at home playing video games or, worse, being bored. The benefit my wife and I enjoy the most is having kids who love to talk freely and honestly about all the good, the bad, and the ugly things we encounter in life.

Too often, we as parents get sidetracked in getting *stuff* for our kids. But when it comes down to it, what kids really want are parents who love them and care for them. The most effective way to show them we love them and care for them is to give them our time and attention.

This is what I learned from my dad in the outdoors, and it's what I love passing on to my own kids. It's a sort of wisdom that doesn't come with, and can't be replaced by, the stuff we buy with a credit card. It only comes from living life together in the outdoors—and the related memories we get to share with generations to come.

Quality time takes time.

DON'T HURRY

It was a warm November day during deer season when I crested the hill ahead of my wife. When I say "hill," I should maybe say butte in the badlands of North Dakota. It was steep, and we were walking cattle trails just to stay vertical ourselves.

Anyway, as I came over the hill, I saw them: a small herd of mule deer. I immediately looked back at Kirsten and started to motion frantically as I mouthed the words "HURRY UP!" She started coming up the hill faster, not knowing what was going on at the top. As she got to me, she was winded from the quick climb as I told her: "Shoot the one on the left."

Needless to say, she missed that mule deer doe that day— because of everything *I* had done wrong. Her glasses were steamed up, she was tired from the climb, and she never had a chance to get in good shooting position. All because *I* was in a hurry. All because I was in a hurry for no reason. The muleys were just hanging out and never saw me. They weren't going anywhere until I made all the noise.

When it comes to raising kids in the outdoors, learning not to hurry isn't just a good idea; it's essential. The consequences can be pretty severe if you don't follow this two-word mantra: "don't hurry," "don't hurry," "don't hurry."

When we hurry, we make mistakes and bad decisions. Worse, we make our kids feel inadequate. Sadly, being in a hurry drives many kids away from the outdoors, and their parents don't understand why.

You're probably wondering to yourself at this point: How, then, do we teach our kids to be swift and action-minded when seconds count during a hunting or fishing trip?

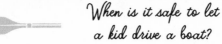

When is it safe to let a kid drive a boat?

A couple of years ago, my son Peter was blessed with a dream opportunity for any seventeen-year-old: driving a demo boat for a local boat dealer. Yep, his job was to take people fishing in a demo boat and show them all the boat's features.

As parents, the question we fielded the most at the time was: "Is it safe to let a kid drive a boat by themselves?" With confidence, we were able to answer: "It's safer than most adults driving a boat." This response sprouted from "don't hurry," and what I started learning on the hill that November day when I was deer hunting with my wife.

When we're teaching the outdoors (or anything else), there are a few principles we need to understand. First, we need to know the capabilities and limitations of the person we're teaching. This is critical, especially when we're teaching hunting. If, for instance, you give most little-framed kids a caliber gun that is too big for them, they will get scared and even get hurt from the kick. This outcome, in turn, can easily lead to lifelong bad shooting habits like flinching and closing their eyes. Far better, then, to find a gun that fits the person you're teaching, give them good hearing protection, and let them learn at their own pace. That's right: "Don't hurry."

Everyone is different. As kids mature, their capabilities change year to year and even month to month. It's important to let them grow into the physical and mental skills they need to succeed in the outdoors. This includes how they hold a rod or a gun. As they grow, they will naturally gain strength and muscle memory that will allow them to be more technical and proficient.

Your example is more important than their capabilities. When we practice what we teach, we instill confidence and reinforce the principles and skills necessary for a fun, safe outdoor experience. I love watching kids mimic the best practices they've learned from their parents. One summer, my oldest son Dan and I were watching a family with young kids struggling to work together in their boat. Dan looked at me and said: "They need to be taught about boat rules." I asked: "Which ones?" I laughed at his answers, because each one he listed he learned by example—not by being told—as he was growing up.

Finally, we all need to take the time to enjoy the outdoors together as a family. Some of my most memorable times with the kids have come about when we've left a tree stand on a dark, clear night. On these occasions, regardless of the homework or chores the kids may still have ahead of them, we lie down in the grass and watch the stars together. We then get to talk over the night's hunt and life in general. It's times like these that build relationships that last a lifetime with your kids. And they're made possible when you're not in a hurry.

The reason I was confident in Peter's solo boating skills, by the way, was that I knew he understood the principle "don't hurry." He had worked on his skills at one mile per hour until he had them down. Then he had worked on them at two miles an hour, and so on. The best part is that now, the kids sometimes look at me and remind me: "Dad, slow down."

The day after Kirsten missed her muley, we found another small group of deer and slowly followed them until we converged on opposite sides of the same draw. We got to the spot first and had the opportunity to find a good shooting position. As the deer came into range, we took the time to watch them interact with each other and their surroundings. Not being in a hurry taught us a lot about mule deer and each other. When she was ready, Kirsten squeezed the trigger—and made the perfect shot.

As you get out with the kids or folks who are new to the outdoors, take the time to learn together and enjoy the experience together. Let skills be built at the speed of each person's pace and capabilities. The definition of success is a positive outdoor experience. Not hurrying makes it possible, and a lot of fun.

It's easier to enjoy family when you're not in a hurry.

Hunting pike is about so much
more than catching big fish.

chapter 9

HUNTING PIKE

I've heard it said that once you have kids, your outdoor life is over. And I'll bet you a jig box that you can't go a week without hearing someone say: "Kids only want to stay inside and play video games."

Well, both of these statements are only as real as we adults make them.

My most memorable outdoor experiences have centered on learning with my kids. I also guarantee you that if you give kids the chance to participate in and enjoy outdoor activities, the majority of them will—heavy emphasis on *enjoy*. Don't believe me? Look at the growth in numbers in youth archery, skeet shooting, and fishing across the United States.

What does all of this have to do with hunting for pike? Too often, we adults get caught up in how things "need" to be done. We focus on teaching only one thing at a time, and we teach that one thing in only a single scenario. Like it or not, when we do this, we are teaching *rules*.

Rules are important where they belong, but they are limiting and harmful where they do not belong. The outdoors is all about *principles* and learning how and when to apply them.

Rules usually start with one of two words: "always" or "never." As adults, we make rules all the time without even being aware of it. One of the many unintended consequences: We steal a kid's chance to enjoy the outdoors.

When we teach our kids principles, on the other hand, we help them enjoy the outdoors, and we get to enjoy it with them. And the side benefit of teaching principles is that we learn more about a topic by teaching it than we would ever expect.

That's why I love teaching kids to hunt for pike. It's not some amazing plan I came up with as a young parent. It's one of the things I've learned from teaching my kids the outdoors. And I learned it because I was teaching someone else. It was something I ended up doing naturally by teaching principles and not rules.

One cool fall day when my oldest boys were in their second year of archery hunting, we were setting up tree stands. One of them asked: "Dad, so we hunt deer just like pike?" The question kind of caught me off guard, but the answer was: "Yep, I guess it's exactly the same." Without realizing it at the time, I had been using the principles I'd learned for hunting to teach the boys how to fish. I also realized that day how many fish I have caught using hunting principles that most anglers never use.

I have always said that what makes me a good fisherman and a bad hunter is my lack of patience. If I'm not catching fish, I'm changing something until I do—with one exception. That exception is when I'm fishing for big pike. I know it takes patience to catch big pike, so it's a good time to bring the kids and have a good time on the water together.

When the kids are on the water with me, the goals are to learn something new, have fun, and hopefully catch a fish or two; pretty easy goals to meet. As part of these outings, the kids have learned how to build and start a fire multiple different ways under less-than-ideal conditions. And once they'd learned how to start a fire, they learned how to cook over one. Staying warm and having a full belly helps with patience.

Peter scored a big fish.
I scored a memory.

Similarly, you can't catch fish if you're in the wrong spot. So we've all learned how pike smell, eat, and see. And we've taken what we've learned and had the boys apply it to reading a map. On the lake map, we look for holes, channels, points, and saddles—places that all the fish in an area get concentrated in as they pass by. This concept is what eventually sparked that question in the field: "Dad, so we hunt deer just like pike?" The boys had put two and two together and realized that holes, channels, points, and saddles are no different than pastures, creek beds, tree lines, and narrows. It doesn't matter if you're fishing or hunting: Topography concentrates what you're looking for. This is an easy lesson to learn on the ice or onshore as you're patiently fishing for pike.

Another important principle that will revolutionize your hunting and fishing success rates is the idea of food vs. instinct. Studying pike, we've learned that they are all about food most of the year. But when the spawn comes, they are about reproduction. Fish aren't smart; they follow food or their instincts. As anglers, then, we need to observe and figure out what the fish are reacting to.

When folks are deer hunting, they call this same concept *patterning* the deer. Over the years, more than 80 percent of our family's archery deer have been shot in the spot the boys picked the day they asked the question: "Dad, so we hunt deer just like pike?" The same is true with nearly all the big pike we've caught. We look at the map and make some predictions about where the fish should be, then identify the spot that will concentrate those fish and give it a try. Sometimes we miss—just like we sometimes miss the deer when we're hunting—but we always meet our goal of learning something new and having fun.

I look forward to hunting pike with my kids every year, for multiple reasons. First off, it's just a lot of fun. Eating, learning, and playing together brings you and your kids closer. I can also say, without any doubt, that I am more successful at hunting and fishing because I get to plan and go pike hunting with my kids every year. Finally, I can safely say that my kids would rather be in the outdoors than at home playing video games—and on a good day, they will now take *me* with *them* so I can learn from them.

What's most important is that my outdoor life isn't *over* because of my kids.

It's *better*.

Sometimes the options seem a little bit confusing.

10

BUILDING A TACKLE BOX

Let's pretend it's December and Christmas is coming. Some of us up north have been ice fishing for a couple of weeks already. The lingering question out there is: What do you put in the stocking and under the tree for your young angler?

Here are some of the principles and ideas I've learned over the years that will shed some light on building a tackle box with the kids in your life.

One of my favorite Christmas gifts ever—and, hands down, the one my mom is still the most upset about—was a book from my aunt entitled *How to Make Your Own Lures and Flies*. The book described how to create fishing lures using all the shiny stuff you find around the house. I was only in fourth grade, but the book poured gas on the passion I had for fishing.

All these years later, I have a family of tackle makers, with my oldest two boys running a successful tackle company. In fact, I wrote this book because, in all fairness, I am riding on the coattails of my son Peter.

One of my mentors once gave me this nugget of wisdom: "Families that fish together fish." This idea is true at the lake and at home. If you want your kids to like fishing when they grow up, they need to be part of the fishing experience *as* kids. Nothing will turn a kid off faster than letting your actions say: "Fishing is for adults, not kids." When this happens, they typically retreat to the things that won't reject them—video games and TV, for example. But when you involve kids in all the activities of fishing, cool things happen. A friend of ours, for example, was working with his son on fishing stuff one winter day when the boy designed a musky bait. The two of them eventually sent the design to a company that couldn't resist making the bait.

I've been saying throughout this book so far that the definition of success in the outdoors is simply having a positive outdoor experience. It starts at home.

When it comes to building a tackle box for kids, start with the basics: hooks, split shot, bobbers, and some jigs. One rule of thumb: Don't give kids anything you'll get upset about when they a) lose it, or b) leave it full of water or sand so that everything rusts between trips. When you're not fishing, have some line and snap swivels around for your kid to practice knots. It makes for a great game on those cold, wet days when you're not out on the water.

As a rule, people take better care of the things they earn. Kids are no different. So have projects and jobs for your kids, outside of daily chores, that they can complete to earn a trip to the bait shop or tackle store—and once there, let *them* pick out the gear they want for their box. Trust me when I say that they won't pick what you would. That's okay.

As my kids have grown up, some of my favorite memories haven't been on the water so much as in the basement, building lures and organizing tackle boxes. Getting to watch our older two teaching the younger ones what they've learned has just been the icing on the cake.

Here are some of our favorite tackle projects:

*Snow days
at the Olson house.*

- **Cheap, plain spoons and white crankbaits** are a lot of easy fun. You can usually find these in clearance racks at some time of the year, which will allow you to stock up with little investment. Use anything you have available to color or paint them. Our favorite approach is to use metallic fingernail polish on the spoons and Sharpies on the cranks. Don't overlook model paint and spray cans, though. Pretty much anything works, as long as it doesn't wash off when it gets wet. One nice thing about fingernail polish: It's easy to take off with nail polish remover, and it's super cheap in most stores. Spinners are also easy to color up and customize—little cost and lots of fun.

- **Bottle cap jigs** are another inexpensive and easy project. All you need are some bottle caps, copper-coated BBs, split rings, and some hooks. Fold the bottle cap in half and place two or three BBs inside. Flatten each end with pliers, then drill or punch a hole in the flat part that is big enough for a split ring and a hook. Color them up and you're ready to catch fish.

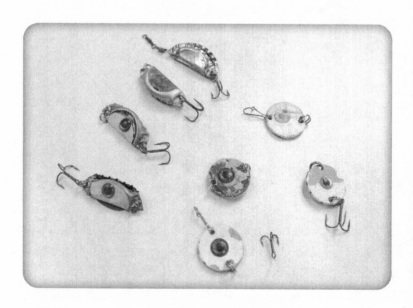

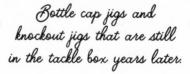

Bottle cap jigs and knockout jigs that are still in the tackle box years later.

- **Knockout jigs** are similar to bottle cap lures, but you use the metal circles that are knocked out of electric panels and boxes. It's best to have a drill press to drill the holes you need. These jigs powder-coat easier because of the heavier metal used to make them. Taking this concept one step further: Any non-rusting metal that can be fashioned into a lure can work. A word of advice, though: Stay away from the utensils in the kitchen drawer. I'm just sayin': It may not go well. Fun, yes. Go well, no.

You see, when you're building a tackle box with kids, it's about learning, ownership, and relationships. It's about making memories and creating joy for everyone involved. The right thing in the box is what the kid wants to put into the box. I'm not saying you give them whatever they want. I'm saying you give them the opportunity to set goals and achieve them—through the many life lessons they'll learn building a tackle box, together with you at home.

Positive experiences X positive memories
= a love of the outdoors.

COLD DAYS AND WARM MEMORIES

When I was a kid, I couldn't wait for a blizzard that would set in big enough to cancel school. If you're older than about thirty-five, you understand how rarely school got called off back then.

Now, you need to realize from the get-go that I'm not writing to take a stand on how wimpy people are in today's society; I'll let all of you talk about that on your own. What I am saying is that school seemingly never got called off when I was a kid. On the rare day when my school's name did show up on the crawling graphic on the bottom of the TV screen, one of two things happened:

- We went outside to play—and when I was in high school, that meant I'd go hunting or fishing. Or ...

- When the weather was so bad that we couldn't even make it out of the farmyard, we went downstairs, started a fire in the wood stove, and spent the day in the family room together.

Nowadays many people put a lot of effort into vilifying or defending technology, the pace of life, kids today, and more. But as I've said before: This isn't about what's happening today. I'm just stating the reality of our culture. And so before I get into the heart of this chapter, I have one request of you. It's a simple one, but it will have a huge impact on how you read the chapter. Are you ready? Here it is:

Please don't spend your time trying to take a side.

Yep, that's it. As you read this chapter, don't look for right or wrong. If you're up for it, keep reading and I'll tell you why at the end. (Oh, and don't cheat and skip to the end to decide if you're going to participate.)

Back to the family room and the wood burning stove on a snow day: What I loved about the cold winter days we spent in front of the stove was that it felt like time was suspended. Not only was school canceled, but so was work for Mom and Dad. You may think that would have been a given, but I grew up with Dad working at home. Yet when a snow day came, everything stopped, including Dad working at home.

Looking back on these warm days over forty years later, while I'm sitting in my own living room with my own kids, there's one thing I know for sure: The days in front of the fireplace are some of the most important days for raising kids. I don't say this lightly. As simple as it is to sit in front of a fireplace on a cold winter day, there's a lot that can happen in the warmth of the fire's flame.

When Mother Nature grants us the opportunity to take a break, it's good to take it. When we as families take that break together, we show each other that we care more about each other than the stuff we do. The sooner this message takes hold in the lives of our kids, the more it builds relationships that last a lifetime.

It also helps put into perspective all the things we spend time on. Put another way: It gives us a chance to balance our relationships. It allows us to stop everything we're doing and focus on the people joined together in front of the fireplace instead of ourselves—which in turn allows us to show that we care.

Another benefit of getting stuck at home in front of a warm fire is that stories get told. Lots and lots of them. Some are funny, others are serious, still others are sad, and a few are maybe better considered confessions, but they're all stories. There's a lot of power in them too, because on those cold days in front of the fireplace when we have our guard down, we can be honest and we have no one to impress.

Looking back over the years, it's amazing how much I've learned about the outdoors—and the rest of life—while sharing around the fire at home on a snow day. It is in this setting that we get to offer stories from each of our perspectives. We also get to revisit old stories with the benefit of another year of life experience.

When you're gathered as a family around a fire all day long, in your pajamas, it's also pretty hard to take yourself too seriously. Without any warning, laughter sneaks into the setting and changes everything. As parents, we are all too prone to squash laughter when it pops up. Don't. Laughing together is healing and freeing for everyone. Let it happen. In fact, help make it happen. Life is too short to be serious all the time, especially on a day in your PJs with your family.

I think it's fair to say that at the age of forty-something, I look forward to snow days more than my kids do. It's the time when, as a family, we get to look back on the year and remember all we've learned, individually and together. It's when we get to talk about how many times it took to hit a deer, who lost the biggest fish, who got the most freaked out when the pheasant jumped up between their legs, along with all the cool stuff that has happened. As parents, my wife and I gain more insight into what the kids are thinking about in life and where they're going in the next year. It's a chance to understand them better so that we can be better parents—all because of a snow day that most folks are complaining about.

When we put aside the idea of being right and trying to have all the right answers—when we allow ourselves to set everything aside on a cold, miserable day—we get to spend precious time with the people in our lives. We create warm memories and build relationships that are rarely broken apart by all the other stuff in life that people worry about.

While you're thinking about all that, I'm going to start getting the homemade hot cocoa mix ready—so that *I'm* ready for the next wonderful snow day.

part two

TEACHING SKILLS

Cold to the touch is just as important
as knowing how to start a fire.

chapter 12

BASIC OUTDOOR SKILLS

On my first trip to the Boundary Waters Canoe Area in northern Minnesota, my friends and I learned a lesson that has stuck with us to this day.

We had gone out fishing, and we were paddling around the myriad islands, paying more attention to the fishing than our location. Without us realizing it, the sun had started to go down. This is not a big deal when you're in your home territory, where you know every nook and cranny. Growing up in North Dakota, as I did, you can see every yard light for thirty miles. But in the BWCA, when it gets dark, it gets *dark*.

It would be fair to say that we got scared and paddled faster to try to get back to camp—the camp we had lost all track of. In hindsight, though, and having talked about the experience around countless campfires over the years, we were okay that night—because of the basic outdoor skills our dads had taught us to that point. Yes, we made a ton of mistakes. But we would have been just fine spiking out (camping somewhere temporarily for the night) if we'd needed to.

Here's the short list of what we knew and what we learned during this experience. What's important to remember is that I'm still learning these skills today as I'm teaching them to my own family.

KNOTS

Knots confuse most adults. The earlier you learn them, the better. And the more you use them, the easier it is to remember them.

One of the things we've learned from teaching our kids knots is that thanks to the popularity of ratchet straps and other tie-down aids, we all use knots less than we once did. Knots our boys knew when they were younger, for example, they have now forgotten. Asking the youngest kids to tie knots this past winter revealed a parenting truth I needed to learn. We spent a lot of detailed time with the older ones and more general teaching time with the younger kids. So in the summer, we're all going to work on knots together around the campfire with some friendly competition.

If you don't know your knots, the Internet is full of great videos and illustrations on the ones you should master. My short list: square knot, clove hitch, taut-line hitch, double half-hitch, bowline, and sheet bend.

One recommendation: As you're teaching knots, use them in an activity that helps kids understand why they should know them. And remember: It's important to be patient; everyone picks up skills at a different pace.

AWARENESS

Being aware of your surroundings is incredibly important, and with the advent of technology it's a skill that needs to be emphasized. But I'm going to be crystal clear on this one so that no one reading misunderstands and continues blaming kids for lacking awareness.

It's a skill that is learned two ways: by example and by opportunity.

As adults, we need to first demonstrate awareness and talk through the process with kids so that they can build their own awareness. More importantly, we need to give kids the freedom to go into the outdoors and play, learn, and observe. Many of us adults are so worried about safety that we hamstring kids by denying them the opportunity to learn outdoor skills. Unfortunately, the outdoor skill that suffers the most from the "safety" fear is awareness.

FIRE

This seems like an easy skill to learn, but there's way more to fire than you may think.

I'll never forget the time my dad and I were hiking in the rain when he said: "Okay, start a fire." I looked at him and explained how everything was wet and no one could start a fire. He then proceeded to the nearest tree, gently picked off the peeled birch bark, soaked the bark in a puddle, collected two handfuls of matchstick-size dead twigs, pulled out a match, and started a fire on the first strike. He demonstrated that day the importance of understanding fire and how to start a fire when you don't need one—so that you can start one when you do.

The essentials where fire is concerned: learning how to start one, contain it, and put it out cold to the touch when you're done—in all conditions, in any season.

FIRST AID

Basic first aid is an important skill that gets people all worked up. The main thing to remember is the word "basic." The first step is to calm yourself and then calm the person you're helping.

Some additional tips: As a family, pick up an old Scout handbook (1980s or older) or Red Cross first aid book and go through cuts, direct pressure, bites, burns, and breaks. Take the time to practice and get comfortable with the *basics*. First aid can be useful in any life circumstance, and the best way to be calm in a situation is to know what to do and who and when to call.

THE BUDDY SYSTEM

Whenever there's a story about some mishap in the wilderness, there are usually a few common denominators. One is that someone was out alone and never told anyone where they were going, their route, or when they'd be back.

In stories with a positive outcome (or an outcome with closure, anyway), you generally find people who had at least one buddy along with them. The buddy system doesn't prevent bad things from happening. But it does provide built-in support for working together to get through a hard time.

Note: It's important to teach that a cell phone doesn't count as a buddy!

RESPECT

It's essential to understand and respect the outdoors and nature. We, as adults, need to realize that it's more important to respect nature than to fear it. Fear leads to irrational decisions that never help in a bad situation. Respecting nature, on the other hand, leads to wise decisions that prevent you from getting into bad situations.

Kids learn respect by example and experience. So when we, as adults, act on or with fear, we prevent kids (and our fellow grown-ups) from learning respect for the power of the outdoors.

That night in the BWCA so many years ago, our dads didn't panic when it got dark. Unlike us, they were confident in the skills they'd taught us to keep ourselves safe if we had to spend the night in the woods. We each had a day pack with us with everything we needed.

One of the dads stayed in camp while the other paddled out to the middle of the lake in front of our campsite, lit a lantern, and waited. I'll never forget coming around a corner, thinking we'd never find our way back, only to see the light in the middle of the lake leading us to a hot meal.

We didn't get scolded that night. Instead, we were asked what we learned.

Fast-forward half a decade: Two of us who'd gotten lost that long-ago evening as kids undertook a twelve-mile night paddle with a severely sick camper to get him to the emergency room. We navigated by compass, counting strokes and reading a map by flashlight. And we were able to succeed because of the basic skills we were taught growing up and the lessons we learned along the way.

It's our responsibility as adults to do the same thing for kids today.

Success is having a positive outdoor experience.

chapter 13

PLANNING
FOR SUCCESS

Everyone tells us to take a kid fishing. There are public service announcements, pro anglers talking about it at the end of their TV shows, online videos, and cool graphics in your favorite magazines urging you to take a kid fishing.

But I'll bet many of you are asking the same question countless other people have asked me over the years. It's a good one, one that *needs* to be asked:

"How do you take a kid fishing?"

Before we get into the plan *we* use, whether it's with kids or new anglers, we need to define "success." When we're talking about kids and people who are new to the outdoors, this is the definition of success we use: a positive outdoor experience.

It doesn't matter how many fish they catch, how big the fish are, or what kind. What matters is that the person has a positive outdoor experience.

To ensure this happens, you first need to plan the trip. Get to know your angler, their attention span, their capabilities, and their limitations. Then pick a lake that fits your angler. Some of *our* favorites are ones that are passed over all the time because they don't have big fish in them.

Take a good look at stunted panfish lakes that are full of four- to eight-inch fish. These lakes are great for young kids with shorter attention spans; they can catch one fish after another, and you can start teaching them catch-and-release as well.

Consider small-pike lakes too. You can generally catch a lot of fish in them consistently, while giving kids the opportunity to learn more-advanced skills. These are great places for kids to learn basic jigging concepts and still be able to catch fish even if they're not doing it quite right.

With kids who are ready for more, start looking for walleye lakes with a good evening bite, as well as big-pike lakes. These settings stretch both skills and attention spans. One thing we like about big-pike lakes is that they offer an opportunity for having a campfire and doing a little cooking and/or playing on the ice—all accompanied by the chance to catch a huge fish.

Great expectations kill the fun in fishing. Not every trip goes as planned. So don't make a big deal out of the trip before you go. That way, the kids won't be disappointed if (when?) the trip doesn't go according to the higher expectations you might have otherwise set.

I like to have a couple of options and pick the one that makes the most sense based on the weather and the mood of the kids that day. You always want to have an alternate plan for bad days, too. My boys loved our "planned tackle-making days," when the weather was too bad to venture out. They never knew the original plan had been to fish that day. They just woke up and had fun in the shop with Dad.

When you get out on the ice in the winter, give kids jobs to do so that they learn how to fish. Throw a wood handle on a skimmer (it will float) so that they can skim holes without worrying about losing the skimmer. Shoveling snow and carrying minnows are other good tasks to assign. Keep the jobs fun, and don't make work out of something the kids will get in trouble for if they do it wrong. My rule of thumb: Get firm with them only on safety concerns, and always explain to them the causes and effects of their actions—along with the consequences—in a calm but stern voice. Then positively get back to fishing.

Have plenty of food and drinks. The rule is: "Never get cold, never get hungry." Warm, full kids have a lot of fun, better energy, and longer attention spans. Cold kids (all cold people!) tell stories of how miserable and boring fishing is. So have more than enough to eat and drink, as well as a place to warm up. I have a lot of great memories of pike tip-up days, sitting in the pickup listening to college football on the radio with the kids.

A Wing-It slip bobber is invaluable when you're fishing with kids. With virtually no effort, you can change bobber size to match what the kids are fishing with. The bobber can easily be taken off and put back on if your angler chooses a different way to fish. It can also be used as a slip or spring bobber, and it's a perfect tool for teaching kids how to jig because it offers a reference point that they can see. Experienced anglers often forget that when a bait stops moving or starts moving, it triggers fish to strike. Using a bobber to teach kids how to jig automatically creates both triggers, which leads to the kids catching more fish.

Make sure you have plenty of warm and extra clothes. One of the rules we have on the ice is: "Don't fall into a hole or get wet." Of course, the kids do fall into holes and get wet. This is not the rule to get mad about. It's one that will save a kid's life when they're older. Ice fishing is a great way for kids to learn the effects of getting cold and wet, and how to be prepared when it happens.

Warm, full kids have a lot of fun.

Make sure you leave before they've had enough. When a kid says "I'm done," "I'm cold," or "I'm bored," it's time to go. Better yet: Watch the kids throughout the experience and call it a day *before* they say they're done. This is more important than you may think. Boredom and/or cold can take a great day on the ice and turn it into a bad experience that a kid remembers for life. Stopping while the memory is positive is crucial to having a positive outdoor experience.

Don't forget to take lots of pictures of your trip. One of the keys to fostering a hunger for the outdoors, in young and new anglers alike, is giving them the tools to tell their story. I have almost as much fun watching young and new anglers talk about everything that went into them catching the fish in the picture—the picture they're using to tell their friends and family all about it!—as I do *taking* them fishing in the first place. Additionally, photos help kids learn how to express themselves and become more relational at a time when it's becoming a lost art.

Remember this above everything else: It's all about having fun so that your angler wants to go fishing again.

I've been using this plan for more than thirty years and tweaking it for every angler I take out, both on the ice and in the open water.

Trust me: It works.

Make sure they're part of the experience.

chapter 14

PICKING THE RIGHT TECHNIQUE

The toughest part about writing this chapter is choosing from the collage of stories I've had the opportunity to live with my kids as they've grown up. The one that sticks out most, though, is a quick shore fishing trip the family made to nearby Lake Audubon many years ago. The kids were seven, five, three, and one at the time, and we were hitting an easy night bite for some small walleye.

It was a perfect scenario. The kids could catch all the fish they could dream of in a short time, and then the quick ride home usually put them all to sleep.

About two weeks into this pattern, the kids were getting it figured out. They would catch fish, measure them, throw the really small ones back, and put the keepers in the bucket.

Then it happened.

Peter heard the bells on the rod ringing. Racing his brother to the rod, he yelled: "It's huge!"

As he pulled the rod out of the holder, it was almost ripped from his hands. You could see the wheels spinning in Peter's five-year-old mind as he struggled to fight the monster on the other end of the line and tried to figure out how to land the biggest fish of his life.

My wife saw him figure it out first. She pointed at him as he turned around and put the rod over his lowered shoulder. And then, with form that would make any football line coach proud, he drove inland.

There's a balancing act between art and science.

When he thought he'd gone far enough, he whipped around and ran back to the shore, reeling as fast as he could. Then he turned back around and repeated the process.

My wife and I laughed as the brothers cheered Peter on. When all was said and done, he had landed a carp that was pushing fourteen pounds. What a night!

When you take a youngster fishing, there's a balancing act between art and science. You need to consider several factors: the child's capabilities, attention span, limitations, and—maybe most importantly—how much they like to fish.

You may already be sick of hearing me say it, but we can't forget the definition of success: a positive outdoor experience. It's all about having fun and learning life lessons together while building relationships.

Picking the right fishing technique for your outing can make or break the day. Here's a primer.

CRANKING

You may be thinking: "This guy has lost his mind, cranking with kids."

Cranking has a reputation it didn't ask for. Many anglers simply overcomplicate it. In my home state of North Dakota, cranking is viewed by many as an expert walleye tactic. What I love about cranking with kids is that you can cover a lot of water and have a chance of catching almost everything.

As my kids were growing up, we would go to small lakes and pull cranks in the canoe for pike. We rarely caught any huge fish. But you can't get the smile off a kid's face when they've just had a seventy-five-fish day with a four-pound average.

When you're in the boat, it's easier for smaller kids to reel with the rod in the rod holder, with limited snags. Cheap cranks on a spinning rod/reel combo are all you need to catch perch, trout, bass, pike, walleye, and—don't forget—white bass.

As the young anglers gain experience and confidence, it's easy to keep stretching them technically so that they learn something new each trip.

RIGGING

When the bite is hot, rigging live bait is very similar to cranking. But it can get complicated and dull quickly. I can't count the hours of boredom I endured as a kid with guys who couldn't find the fish, got mad at all the snags, and fill in the blank with every other horror story you've ever heard. We've all been there.

Even when you're using rod holders, rigging takes a bit more skill than many of us think. You might be saying: "Olson's never fished before. How can you screw up a bottom bouncer and a spinner?" Well, here's my answer: You know that guy who knows everything, but has never been fishing in a boat before and everything goes wrong? As simple as rigging is, it's a lot for new anglers to comprehend and put into practice. When I was teaching my kids to rig, we always shared a rod until they'd figured out each aspect of the technique. Once kids start to master the necessary rod handling skills, though, rigging is a great way for them to learn fish behavior and locations.

BOBBERS

I'm getting to that point in life when people are telling me I should start acting my age. But is it my fault if I can't help getting excited about little things like a bobber slowly submerging out of sight?

Red-and-white bobbers and kids are iconic. But casting a traditional bobber is tough. Choosing a slip bobber and a small jig is definitely the way to go, especially when kids are learning how to cast. There's also less chance of needing to learn how to remove a hook from your kid's skin.

Err on the side of numbers of fish, not size of fish.

One of the mistakes I made with my own kids was trying to wean them off bobbers once they were "old enough." But like everything else in fishing, we need to use the technique that catches fish. One summer, when they were in high school, the boys and I were at a fishing retreat on Devils Lake in northeastern North Dakota. It was three days of nonstop catching—and yep, it was all on bobbers.

Like cranking, bobbers are super simple. But as your kids' skill levels increase, you can implement some pretty elaborate bobber tactics. Don't overlook big bobbers and bait for pike and catfish. The fishing might be a little slower, but your kids' smiles will most certainly be bigger.

SHORE FISHING

When it comes to shore fishing, we're spoiled in the Dakotas. There are countless miles of shoreline you can pull up to and fish, with almost any kind of structure (drop-offs, rip-rap, trees, weedlines, etc.) you can dream of.

What's nice about shore fishing with kids is that you can have lines in the water while playing catch, working on knots, having a campfire, or doing whatever else keeps the kids occupied between catching fish. My kids love capturing frogs for bait and catching big smallies and pike—while eating their weight in brats and s'mores.

Shore fishing is great for the whole family because regardless of fishing interest, there's always something to do. It's also fun to watch a disinterested youngster's shell crack when, suddenly, they're reeling in a fish they didn't care about minutes before.

My kids are far from little now, but I still can't wait to get out and shore fish with them in the fall. It's one of my favorite settings to talk and work on other outdoor skills.

THE THOUGHT PROCESS

Regardless of the outdoor activity you choose for kids, picking the right technique for the day boils down once again to four key considerations: each kid's capabilities, limitations, attention span, and interest.

Don't feel bad about taking a kid out individually for a trip that fits their *specific* capabilities and interests. It's better to go out one on one sometimes instead of taking the whole crowd with their differing attention spans and abilities. Fishing within their capabilities helps kids catch fish and have fun while they're doing it.

Going through this process when they're young is a good way to prepare kids for future outdoor activities as they mature. Don't make things complicated. Just take the time to be deliberate in your decision making, so that everyone will have a better chance of having a positive outdoor experience.

Bobbers are for more than just staring at.

BOBBERS
AND KIDS

It was a hot summer day, and I'll admit my patience was pretty low. But I still took the kids to one of our favorite shore fishing spots for a night of fishing and a campfire.

Our son Peter was about three at the time and was showing his independence every chance he could get. We were bobber fishing on this trip, for several reasons—one of which was the fact that when you're bobber fishing, lines are easy to keep track of and the kids can see the bobber go down, adding to their excitement.

On this night, though, Peter had something else in mind.

Every time I went to help one of the other kids, Peter would reel in his line. It wasn't a slow, methodical retrieve, either. It was more of a NASCAR-crossed-with-a-marlin-charter, light-the-water-on-fire retrieve. So each time Peter brought in his line, I explained to him that if he wanted to catch fish, he needed to leave the bobber out where the fish were.

On my tenth or so attempt to get my point across to this budding young angler, something horrible happened. You know what I'm talking about: It's the thing that gets in the way when you're trying to convince your kids of something.

Peter caught a fish.

And not just any fish, mind you. It was a two-and-a-half-pound smallie.

That's right. I was wrong.

What made it even worse was that my wife took Peter's side—and used my own words against me—when she said: "Isn't it about having fun? Let him fish how he wants to." It takes a lot out of a guy when both your wife and your three-year-old are right on the same day.

At the end of the night, Peter had just under a three-pound average with four smallies, and he topped things off with an assortment of other fish using his speed-demon retrieve.

Most of what I've written in this chapter are bobber tactics I've learned fishing with Peter as he's grown up, and that I have refined with our other kids as well as with new anglers.

Bobber fishing is one of the simplest traditional tactics out there. With just a few variations, you can be extremely adaptable to some pretty technical situations. That's why bobbers are so important when you're teaching people how to fish. And along the way, you'll learn—like I have—some lessons about fish that you never would have guessed you'd learn.

Not all bobbers are created equal. So you need to pick through the options to make the right choice for the conditions you're going to encounter. I break bobbers down into four categories: traditional *round* bobbers, *spring* bobbers, *slip* bobbers, and *combination* bobbers.

- **Traditional round bobbers** are inexpensive and provide a lot of buoyancy. You can put them on a line and take them off easily. But they're hard to cast with more than a couple of feet of line, which makes them *really* hard to cast for kids with shorter rods. The buoyancy is also a drawback when you're fishing for sensitive fish that feel the bobber and let go. Made of hard plastic, these bobbers also tend to break easily on rocks. And the internal spring likes to rust after use.

- **Spring bobbers** are typically made of foam, cork, or wood and are long and skinny in shape. They attach to the line by the tension of the spring and the groove in the bottom of the bobber. They offer less resistance when a fish starts pulling on them. They come in a wide range of prices and styles, allowing you to pick the one that works best for you. The drawback of the spring bobber is similar to that of the traditional round bobber: It's hard to cast when you're fishing more than a foot or so below the bobber.

- **Slip bobbers** look very similar to spring bobbers and come in countless options. The difference is that there's a tube running through the slip bobber that your line can slide on. You place a bead and bobber stop on the line, and you can cast and fish as deep as you want with a bobber that reels up to within a couple of inches of the hook. Slip bobbers also tend to be a little more durable and can handle kids better. Their main drawback: You have to cut the line to take these bobbers off or put them on.

- **Combination bobbers** are bobbers that can connect to the line or act as a slip bobber. These bobbers are nice because you can fish with them many different ways without buying multiple bobber styles. The drawback is that they don't have the finesse each of the other bobbers has. That is easily overlooked when you're fishing with kids, as you will see.

The iconic picture of a kid with a traditional round bobber is something we've all seen. When you're fishing with kids in a place where you can use a cane pole or where the depth is a foot of line or less below the bobber, traditional round bobbers or spring bobbers are tried and true for catching panfish and bullheads. But as soon as you start getting deeper than eighteen inches, it's time to switch over to a slip bobber. This strategy will save on tangles, prevent hooks from being stuck in bushes and body parts, and lead to more fish getting caught.

There are a lot more ways to use bobbers effectively, as Peter has taught us, and this is where combination bobbers shine. When you're fishing in a body of water that has a lot of rocks or weeds, you can use a bobber for depth control to stay above the snags. What's nice about this option is that you can get kids used to how fast they need to reel in to stay out of the snags. When they start getting confident, you can take the bobber off and let them try it without assistance.

This is also a great way to fish rivers with jigs. The kids can cast and retrieve, letting the current and their reeling move the jig, again keeping it out of the snags. I've used this technique with spoons, inline spinners, jigs, cranks, and anything else the kids could put on the line.

When you're teaching kids (and even adults) how to vertical jig, try using combination bobbers as an aid. Set the bobber stop just above the bottom and have your young angler jig with the goal of keeping the bobber flat on the surface. As they progress, you can take the bobber off and let the kid use the bobber stop as a guide to see if they're keeping the line tight enough. The beauty of this technique: When the kid gets bored or gives up, the jig hangs in the strike zone and a lot of times triggers a strike. The other nice thing about using combination bobbers with kids is that as you change lure sizes, you can change bobber sizes as well in no time at all.

Let's not forget the speed-demon bobber retrieve! Skipping bobbers across the surface has put a lot of pike, bass, and even walleye in the bucket for us over the years, despite my previous ignorance. That bobber doesn't have to just sit there. It can do a little movin'.

So when you're out fishing with kids, make sure you have some bobbers on hand—and that you let the kids get creative so that you can all catch more fish and have more fun.

You got to fish where the fish are.

PICKING
THE RIGHT LAKE

I love listening to conversations between my boys and adults who ask the loaded question every novice angler and even accomplished fisherman can't help but ask:

"How do you catch so many fish?"

The boys' typical response is an Al Lindner bit of wisdom: "You got to fish where the fish are." The questioner then chuckles and says: "Well, okay, if that's all you're going to tell me, then you're growing up to be a fisherman for sure."

What's funny about my boys' advice is that a lot of times, fishing really *is* that simple. Kids catch more fish when you put them in a spot where there *are* fish. The boys are right; Al just might be on to something.

One of the main goals in taking a kid or new angler fishing is to catch some fish! The key to achieving that goal is picking a lake with fish that fit the needs of the angler you're taking out that day. Putting a little bit of energy into choosing the right water for your outing usually determines whether it will be a fun trip or a story about sitting around being bored.

Look for kinds of water and kinds of fish—not specific species or destinations. Here's what I mean. When I'm picking a place to take a young angler fishing, I'm looking for a setting that fits their ability level and attention span and stretches them at the same time. Focusing on a particular species of fish greatly reduces the opportunities and fun the child can have on the trip.

Here's what you can do instead.

First, consider a stunted lake that is full of four- to eight-inch panfish, eight- to fourteen-inch walleye, or twelve- to twenty-four-inch pike. These lakes are great for young kids with shorter attention spans because they can catch countless fish, one after the other. These settings also give you the chance to start teaching the hows and whys of catch and release. Best of all, these lakes are usually everywhere, making them easy to get to.

Next, look at small ponds and lakes where the fisheries folks put in nearly grown fish for anglers to easily take. You can generally catch nicer fish in these areas consistently, all while giving kids the opportunity to learn more-advanced skills. Offering a little bit of everything—walleye, trout, cats, bass, panfish, and more—these areas are great places for kids to learn basic concepts and catch fish, even if they're not always doing things quite right.

Most people avoid rivers, fearing snags and perceived difficulty. But rivers give young anglers the opportunity to be surprised by every catch; you just never know what you're going to pull out. Another plus to rivers: They're full of barriers that congregate fish. Jetty and dam hopping up and down rivers provides both an adventure and fish.

River fish are also less affected by the weather, but they respond to current speed and water levels. This makes predicting where they'll be and when they'll be biting a bit easier. So think of the river as a great backup plan if the weather doesn't cooperate for your lake adventure.

Finally, there's big water. When it comes to big water, you'll generally find an abundance of published information on what's going on with fish location and how the fish are biting. Once you find fish, big water provides *bigger* fish. But those fish can take more time and technical skill to catch. On good days, big water is great for any angler. But on average or slow days, it's better suited for kids who have patience and more technical skills.

Big water has one big advantage: options. Some of my happiest fishing memories are of getting into huge schools of hungry goldeyes, drum, white bass, or catfish with the kids. It's like fishing in a stunted lake, but with a one- to two-pound average. It's not just fun; it's the experience that will be talked about forever.

Access will ultimately rule the day. If you pick the right body of water but you can't get to the fish, well, then you've picked the wrong body of water.

Now, when I say access, I'm not just talking about the lake with lots of cabins and a single fishing pier. Access means access to the fish when you're there—and, more importantly, for the young angler you take out that day. A small pond with thirty yards of weeds around the edge puts a damper on a shore fishing outing. So when you're choosing a body of water, look at all the access factors: shore fishing or boat, boat size, tackle on hand, experience, and fish location. Don't make things harder than they are. Look at what you have and know, then pick a lake that fits and has access to the fish that day.

Timing is more important than most people think. I can't count the number of times I've heard someone say: "Well, we caught fish there last month." Fish follow food and instincts. If you fish in the same place all the time, you'll have some good days and more bad days. Why? Because you won't always have access to the fish where you're at.

So when you're picking a body of water and a specific place to fish there, you need to look at the fish movements and behaviors. A family tradition of ours is shore fishing at a local big body of water in the fall during pheasant season. The walleye and smallies are up close to shore, and we can spend the night relaxing around the fire while we're catching our limits of fish. But fish that same place in the summer and you'll catch almost nothing.

Spring and fall are generally good times to cast spinners and spoons on trout ponds. But in the heat of the summer, trout dough is the only way to go in those same places.

Don't worry: You don't need to figure all of this out on your own. There's lots of help available. You just need to ask.

There are many resources to help you pick the right body of water. Contrary to popular belief, the pros are using the same resources you have access to. There aren't too many secrets out there; you just need to know where to look.

Start with your state's DNR or game and fish website. Most states have interactive maps that cover lake contours, stocking reports, fish size and status, and more. Take this information and combine it with information from companies that have fishing maps you can download to your phone. You'll then have a good start on picking the right lake for your next trip.

Ask around amongst the people you know, too. Yes, you'll always find the guy who's tight-lipped about everything. But any outdoorsman worth anything will help you find a good place to take new anglers to catch fish. This includes, by the way, the pros in your area. Message them and ask for recommendations and ideas. It's their job to help people catch fish, so don't be afraid to seek them out. (Now, all of this comes with the same warning as before: Don't ask about taking kids out and then use the information you get for another purpose.)

Finally, go to the small local bait shop and buy your bait, a snack, and some gas. Yes, it may be more expensive than the box store down the road. But you're there for more than just bait and tackle. You're there for information, and to build a relationship with someone who cares about you and your trip.

Don't forget to say thank you for the information you get. One of the best ways to do so is with a picture of the catch from your day. Size and numbers don't matter; kids with smiles and fish do. So say thanks and send a picture to those who help you out.

Remember: The goal is for your young angler to have a positive outdoor experience on every trip. By taking some time to pick a body of water that matches the angler, you can fish where the fish are and have an adventure that will be talked about for a lifetime.

Kids grow out of life jackets and fishing rods.

17

PICKING THE RIGHT ROD

One day I was down by the river, shore fishing with some friends. Everyone seemed to be catching fish—except for the poor guy with the bad luck. You know the guy: the one who couldn't net a fish in a trout pond at a sport show, even if his life depended on it.

I went over to see if I could help him out and, hopefully, end his night with a little dignity and confidence.

"What do you have on?" I asked.

"Let me show you," he replied.

He then proceeded to reel up his line. It took him about three seconds. Yep, three seconds. He had maybe eight to twelve feet of line out, max.

"Well, there's your problem," I said. "Just cast a little farther out and you'll be on the fish."

It was then that I saw the funniest, most dangerous, but admittedly somewhat intriguing casting technique I have ever witnessed. It covered about six feet. Now I knew what the problem really was: This poor guy was not only fishing with the wrong rod; he'd never been taught how to cast. So for the next half-hour or so, I worked with him to produce a cast that was good enough to catch fish. Mission accomplished.

The trouble with this story is that you can put most kids who are learning how to fish in this guy's shoes, and for the same reason: They're using the wrong rod. When you're teaching someone how to fish, there are a few things to consider when you're picking out a rod that fits their abilities. It's time well spent, because not matching the rod to the angler usually leads to disappointment, frustration, and, in this guy's case ... no fish.

First things first: The guy was using a super flimsy, bend-it-in-a-circle rod. A rod with a slow action and light power is harder for kids to break and is usually cheaper, too. That's why so many new anglers are stuck starting out with this kind of rod. But like the guy in our story found out, these rods can be very difficult to cast.

My rule of thumb for rod action is to start with a fast-action model that is medium/heavy power and see how it fits in the angler's hands. Have them go through some basic casting motions to see how the rod bends. What I'm looking for is a rod that is stiff enough so that the rod does the work, yet also soft enough so that the angler isn't snapping the line or throwing bait off when they cast. I've found that when it comes to figuring out what kids need, it's easier to watch an angler going through casting motions than to look at the manufacturer's claims on a rod. What you'll find most of the time is that a new angler learns to cast faster, and with better accuracy, when you take the rod's stiffness into consideration.

The next question to answer: What's the right length for the rod? Most people have the fond, cute memory of kids and short, beginner rods. But think about watching kids try to fish with those things: Hooks are flinging everywhere, and adults are having to cast for safety's sake.

Casting with a short rod is hard. If you don't believe me, here's a fun experiment: Pull out some panfish ice rods and have an accuracy competition with the family in the backyard.

I like to start out with a rod that is one to one and a half inches taller than the angler, until the angler is five feet tall. For most kids, these mechanics work out best with both the weight and size of the rod and the kid's arm length. An additional benefit is that the hooks on the line are usually far enough away that you don't need to become proficient at hook removal.

When it comes to reels, there's a little more to consider. The old standby spin casting reel that most anglers grew up with is what people tend to think of first. But as we've been talking about, you need to look at the capabilities and limitations of each young angler as your starting point.

The common thought is that spin casting reels are easiest to learn. Most spin casting reels are big and bulky, making them hard to cast and reel for kids with smaller hands. Small spinning reels, on the other hand, are easier for those kids to hold.

Line twist, tangles, and drag are other factors you need to consider when you're picking out a beginner's reel. I have found that, dollar for dollar and time for time, spinning reels are the better option because of their durability. But the reality is that everyone is different, which means they all learn in different ways and times. So you need to help each angler make a good decision *for them*. Expect some trial and error.

Let's talk a little bit about price. Figuring out how much you're going to spend on a rod and reel goes far beyond budget. Considering what we've talked about already, it doesn't matter how much you spend on the rod and reel. If it doesn't fit the angler, it's a waste of money.

Another thing to consider is how much you're willing to spend when the rod tip is broken ... or when the reel no longer works because it was dragged through the sand ... or when any of the other incredibly destructive things kids do to rods and reels happens during the learning process. I don't have any hard numbers, but my rule of thumb is this: I want to spend as much money as necessary to get a rod and reel that is durable enough for at least one fishing season. After all, kids grow, and it probably won't fit next year anyway.

On the flip side of the coin, I don't want to spend so much money that I get angry when the rod and/or reel is broken. There's nothing more tragic than watching a kid hate fishing because they've gotten chewed out for breaking a rod during the learning process. Remember: The goal is for new anglers to have a positive outdoor experience, each time out. Spending the right amount of money on a rod and reel influences this goal more than most people think.

Exception to the rule: Everything we've talked about so far focuses on what it takes to pick out a rod and reel for a kid so they can learn how to cast and catch fish effectively, on their own and at any age. But when it comes to new anglers, especially little ones, my favorite rod-and-reel combo is the six-and-a-half- to seven-foot rod with a bait casting reel in the boat and a spinning reel onshore. These options let small kids reel while leaving the rod in the rod holder. When you're shore fishing, for example, the kid can sit on the ground and reel. In the boat, they can stand and reel. Either way, they get started with the basic hand-eye coordination they need to eventually take the next step of getting their own rod and reel and casting by themselves.

Finally, you need to get some fishing line on the reel. When it comes to new anglers, I'm a big fan of cheap monofilament. I generally go with six- to ten-pound test, depending on what species we're targeting. Mono breaks easily when you need it to, and it's less likely to cut a kid's hands when they're pulling on snags. It's also cheaper to replace when big tangles happen. And trust me: They will happen, regardless of what reel you're using. Mono also makes it easy for kids to practice tying knots, and you don't need any special tools to cut it.

So as you're hitting the sporting goods store to pick out a new rod and reel, keep in mind what your young angler's capabilities are and what it takes for them to have a positive outdoor experience. You'll find that a lot of the lessons you learn choosing appropriate fishing gear for your kids will also help you pick out the right hunting gear for them as they grow.

Shooting with your kids
begins long before hunting season.

18

SHOOTING CLAYS

I'll never forget the first time I had the opportunity to nervously say "pull" and hear the sound of the spring on the thrower, rapidly hurling that little clay disk through the air.

To be honest, I can't be sure if I was more concerned about missing or about having my friends make fun of me if I missed. Either way, I hit that first clay pigeon. And of course—for those of you who have been there—I missed the next nine.

Fast-forward a bunch of years, and I've had the chance to relive that same mix of excitement and fear with all four of my own kids, along with countless other new shooters.

There's something magical about shooting clay pigeons with kids. I'm not sure if it's the anticipation, the excitement when they hit their first pigeon, or the confidence and pride they have after each shot. Whatever it is, it's a lot of fun when done right, and it's an important building block to raising kids in the outdoors.

In reality, shooting with your kids begins long before you actually go out and shoot the first time. There are some basic life principles and mindsets you need to instill in them before you pull out the guns. The short list:

- Teaching them how to trust.

- Helping them realize and accept that there are absolutes.

- Showing them they have responsibilities.

- Making sure they understand the idea of stopping without questioning why.

When you're raising kids, you need to know their abilities and limitations and work with them at their own pace, giving them responsibility as they earn it. Remember: No one can be responsible without the freedom to make their own decisions. Responsibility doesn't come with age; it comes with experience. That's another reason why I love shooting pigeons with my kids. It's a simple way to have all the control you need to teach them step by step and then convert that control to responsibility. It's an activity that builds confidence in kids and parents alike.

The other thing that's nice about shooting pigeons is that it's still relatively inexpensive. Whether you go to a range or put together your own setup, you're not sinking a ton of money into the experience. You can get into a good thrower for under fifty dollars, and pigeons and shells are still about eight to ten dollars per twenty-five rounds.

This past summer, we started going to a nearby gun range with some friends. The range is a great option if you're learning to shoot clays yourself or your kids are to the point where they need to have what you're teaching reinforced by an outside authority. My kids shoot at the range for about the same cost as when we shoot on our own. I recommend just stopping in and asking for a tour with your kids. That way, you can check out the rules and costs and plan an outing. Any good range will be welcoming and excited to help teach your kids.

Kids need to be comfortable and confident with their guns.

Picking the right gun for kids is tougher than you may think, yet easier than many people make it. It's important to pick a gun that fits well and isn't too light. Yep, not too *light*. The lighter the gun, the more kick it has—and using a gun with a heavy kick is the fastest way for a new shooter to pick up a flinch for the rest of their life. I've seen many kids get kicked by a lightweight gun and never want to shoot again. I never truly appreciated this myself until I helped sight in a friend's lightweight youth model

.30-06. At 280 pounds, I have never hurt so much after being kicked by that tiny little gun.

I like to get a gun that is light enough for the kid to hold up but heavy enough to minimize the kick. Shorter barrels and heavier stocks helped with the balance with my own kids.

It's conventional wisdom to start with a .410, which is easy to shoot as far as weight and kick go. But a mentor of mine gave me this advice when I was picking out a gun for my kids to shoot pigeons: "Get the heaviest 20 gauge you can, unless they can hold a 12 gauge," he said.

I, like you just now perhaps, asked: "Whhyyy?"

He then explained to me that it's all about the number of shot in the air. A .410 takes the most skill to shoot. But anyone can hit a pigeon with a 12 gauge. Sure enough, he was right. I still can't hit a pigeon with a .410, but I do pretty well with the old 12 gauge I bought when I was twelve.

So here's where I stand: The most important thing to remember about picking out a gun for kids is that they need to be comfortable and confident with it when they pull the trigger.

When it comes to throwers, I like to stay away from hand throwers when I'm out with kids. Yes, they're cheap, and they're easy to toss into the truck, too. But they take away from your ability to work side by side with your kids while they're shooting. With an inexpensive mechanical thrower, you can consistently throw pigeons one specific way and work on that shot. And once you get that shot down, you can work on the next one. I use a marker or fingernail polish on the thrower to replicate throws from one shot to the next. I've seen some people use electrical tape too. My goal is to have the kids start with a familiar shot to gain confidence, then work on the shots they struggle with.

Make sure, by the way, that you finish each shoot with your kid successfully hitting a few pigeons so that the outing ends on a positive note. (This is a good routine for us adults as well.)

The thing I appreciate most about shooting clays with kids are the endless lessons we experience as a family gathered around that thrower. We learn about competition, encouragement, coordination, and respect, just to get started.

There is one principle, one overarching mindset, that makes these lessons possible, ensures a positive experience, and leads to safe outdoor excursions for life. That principle is:

Slow and steady.

As adults, we need to live slow and steady so that we can model it to our kids. When we hurry, mistakes happen. And when we're using firearms, simple mistakes can have harsh consequences.

Shooting during the summer, slow and steady, makes for memorable days of learning lessons as a family. The benefits of these lessons will be evident in the field each fall—and for the rest of our lives.

When it comes to shooting and teaching,
we learn by example.

GUN RANGE BASICS

A few years back, I was confronted by a gentleman who felt it necessary to let me know that I was taking my kids to the gun range at way too young an age.

Your brain is probably overloading with questions right now, for him and for me. How old were the kids? Who does he think he is? What *is* the right age? Doesn't he understand that this way of thinking is the problem? Does he know the kids? Is he right?

Fill in the blanks with your own questions. In fact, take some time to write them down.

Now that you have your questions out of your head ... let's take a look at gun range basics.

This chapter is not a step-by-step gun range safety list. It simply takes the basic concepts we've been talking about from a fishing perspective and applies them to hitting the range. We all need to understand these principles when we're teaching new shooters of any age. The concepts are rooted in the foundations of safe gun handling skills, but they *DO NOT* take their place.

Regardless of whether you're shooting at a constructed range or out in your backyard at the farm, consider your setting a range and follow all the necessary safety rules.

DEMONSTRATE DISCIPLINE

As adults, we tend to default to scaring safety into kids. This usually involves overreactions and raising our voices, along with big, bad, scary stories.

Don't do that.

We all learn by example. Kids will naturally follow your lead. The key is to explain your actions—factually, calmly, and at the kid's level of understanding. It's pretty simple: The shooter you're teaching will be calm and disciplined if *you* are calm and disciplined. If you're careless and frantic, on the other hand, bad things will happen.

Remember: It's more important to be a good example than to nag on safety.

MEET THEM WHERE THEY ARE

Understanding the capabilities and limitations of your young shooter is important for many reasons.

First, if you push or allow them to try a task that is beyond their capabilities, you introduce bad habits. The most common one involves shooting a caliber, loud, or lightweight gun that scares or hurts them; it can take years to overcome the flinching that results.

You also need to make sure that the gun fits the shooter. An oversize or undersize gun promotes a bad shooting stance. Focusing on consistency in form and breathing, rather than accuracy, reduces the stress the shooter might be feeling about hitting the target. Set up targets at a range that young shooters are comfortable with, then increase distance to match their growing capability.

Finally, don't rush kids to take a shot. It's more important to let them talk through the individual actions they're going to take so that you can reinforce proper shooting technique and decision-making skills. It's better to practice this and *not* go to the range than for a shooter to have an experience that hurts or scares them. Most of the time, you never find out about such things until later in life because kids are usually trying to please you and do a good job.

QUALITY SHOOTS

Growing up, I remember the days we would go out back on the farm and shoot all day long. We would shoot every gun we had, and the bruises we wore showed it.

When I started shooting with my own kids, I realized how many bad habits I had developed thanks to the years of mega shoots. It's more important to have shorter, high-quality trips to the range that improve kids' skills than it is for them to take lots of shots.

The key to a quality time *at* the range is not the quantity of shots; it's the quality of each shot. When young shooters focus on shooting with good form and without fatigue, they build muscle memory that leads to natural, safe gun handling for life. (This is also true, by the way, when it comes to archery.)

MAKE IT REAL

As your shooter progresses in their abilities, you can start working them into more shooting positions. When it comes to hunting, focus on positions they'll encounter in an upcoming hunt. If you'll be hunting out of a ground blind, for example, practice shooting out of that blind. If you'll be hunting out of a tree stand, find a place to put up a tree stand and shoot from there. You will benefit just as much as your young shooter does!

There are lots of little details you take for granted that kids don't yet know. By practicing in a controlled, daylight situation, you can teach them the nuances they'll need to understand to have a successful hunt.

The same goes for clothing. Having kids shoot while they're dressed in their hunting gear looks funny in July. But it instills confidence during the hunt itself.

NO MISTAKES

Ask my kids what happens if you make a mistake with a gun and you will get this answer:

"There are no mistakes, just bad decisions."

It's the same answer you'll get from them if you ask them about making a mistake while driving a car or running a log splitter.

We need to remember not to freak out about guns. There are lots of things in this world that will get someone seriously hurt or killed if we make the wrong decision about them. It's important for us as parents not to make one dangerous thing scarier than another.

Teaching kids to respect and understand the things that can hurt them, or others, will make them safer in the long run. More specifically, the lessons kids learn at the gun range carry over to every other area of their lives. The things my own kids learned at the range when they were young made watching them learn how to drive far less stressful for my wife and me! All because many of the safety principles were already there.

STAY ON TARGET

Practicing at the range teaches young shooters how to hunt properly and responsibly when they're out in the field. It's our job to evaluate them and allow them to prove to us—and, more importantly, to themselves—that they have mastered the skills they need to safely progress. To do this, we need to let them earn the responsibility and demonstrate the proper gun handling skills to move on.

So, getting back to those questions we started with ...

It doesn't matter how old a person is. What matters is how responsible they are and what their skill set is. Responsibility comes from experience, not age. Every kid is different and needs to be allowed to progress at their own pace. The goal is to have fun and learn together, not meet a deadline. The time you spend with kids at the range is far more valuable than how they shoot.

Florence the Confidence Decoy
isn't just for duck hunting.

YOUTH DEER HUNTING

In many northern states, September and October means youth hunting seasons. Many of these seasons are easy to get ready for, but youth deer season takes a little more prep, both on the logistical and the mental side—for parents, not so much kids.

I loved taking my kids out for their first deer hunts. Keeping a few things in mind will help you make these trips positive lifelong memories.

One of the most important things to remember when you're taking kids out on any hunt is to not set any expectations other than to have a safe, fun hunt. Every kid is different, and in this case, you're taking them out on a trip for a first-time experience. When the time comes, some kids will pull the trigger without hesitation. Others will be afraid to shoot. It's critical for the kid you're hunting with to understand that it's okay to shoot and it's okay not to. Looking back, I can't tell you how beneficial this advice was with my own kids.

I will never forget my oldest son Dan's first and second youth deer hunts. Dan was a polished shooter by age twelve; he had a tight two-inch group at 150 yards off-hand with his rifle. So I was not surprised by what he did on his first-year hunt when a doe walked in at 85 yards: He pulled up, went through the paces, and dropped his deer with one shot. When we recovered it, though, Dan saw that his shot was a little high and he had damaged some of the meat. I thought nothing of it, and all was good for the year until the next youth season.

This time, when a doe walked out and stood broadside, Dan couldn't shoot. Even with all his successful practice during the summer, he was so nervous about shot placement that he couldn't pull the trigger.

"It's okay," I whispered into his ear. "There will always be another deer."

A couple trips later, he got his deer and all was well and good once again.

Now that I've hunted with all four of my kids, I can say that each of them has had some sort of reaction I didn't anticipate. But they were ready to handle these challenges because my only expectation for the hunt in each case was to be safe and have fun.

One of the hardest things for us adults to deal with during a youth hunting outing is the fact that it is the *kid's* hunt— and therefore the *kid's* standards that matter. I speak from experience here. I took a week off of work one year so that I could hunt muleys with one of the boys for the youth buck season. We had a place with big muleys we could hunt, and I was stoked with the hope of watching my son get a deer bigger than anything I'd ever shot.

But forty minutes into the season, when a five-by-five whitetail walked in at forty yards, my son pulled up and shot. When

I asked him why he didn't wait for a big muley, he grinned as he replied: "It's bigger than my brother's." That was his standard—and I got to go back to work that week.

A good friend called me last year and asked what to do: His daughter wouldn't shoot a doe because it may have a fawn. My answer was easy: "Bring a camera and a rifle. Let her choose." If we, as adults, push our personal goals, the kids we're hunting with won't grow in their own outdoor experiences.

Youth season is about decision making.

It's hard to pick one hunt over another, but one of my favorite hunting experiences happened when my son Peter was in a tree stand with his uncle—who we were teaching how to hunt—and Peter shot his first buck with a bow. It was only a basket rack, but Peter dropped it all by himself while he was talking his uncle through what he was doing. All the while, I was in a stand twenty yards away, watching with a critical eye. Kids need to learn when to shoot and when not to shoot with our mentoring and our help, not our pressure.

Don't get a gun for a kid, sight it in, and go hunting in the same week. It's a bad idea for an adult, so why would it work for a kid? Find a weapon that won't kick too much for the ability and size of the kid. I prefer to start this process in May, but there are some years when kids grow really fast— so you may need to start practicing as late as August with a gun that fits them.

Practice often with hunting rounds but limit the kid to four to ten shots per trip. Shooting more rounds with a smaller caliber, before or after shooting the hunting practice rounds, helps with hand-eye coordination and proper muscle memory. Shooting lots of hunting rounds, on the other hand, leads to fatigue and flinching, both of which are hard habits to break. I know many adults who struggle to this day because of experiences they had as kids. So more trips to the range with fewer rounds helps a lot. It also leads to a better hunt and better memories.

When it comes to youth hunts, you need to understand each kid's desires, abilities, and limitations. As you plan the hunt with your kids, keep these things in mind. Stretch them enough to grow, but not so much that you leave them with a bad memory. Let them help make decisions on where to go and what to do. If it doesn't work, you can talk about why together. Youth hunting is about learning and about learning together. The one thing I've learned is that deer are less affected by sound than I thought. So answer questions *when they come up*. It's better to spook a deer and answer a question than to shush a kid and have them not learn.

Finally, don't get mad or disappointed about how the hunt goes. Yes, it's a bummer to eat a tag. But if you show any disappointment, I guarantee you that your kids will take it personally, whether you think so or not. We're hunting youth season to help our kids learn and to make memories with them. How can that be disappointing?

Our job as parents is to be there to teach our kids, celebrate with them, encourage them, and everything in between. So get out and practice with your kids. Enjoy your time together so that you can have a memorable youth deer season. It's so much fun.

Never get cold, never get hungry.

chapter

21

WINTER BASICS

Life in the outdoors is about learning and expanding our knowledge of basic skills and principles. We all need to start at our ability level, stretch ourselves with help, and continue to improve on our outdoor capabilities. It doesn't matter how old you are; it's the same for everyone.

It's easier, though, to learn outdoor skills as a kid. And when it comes to winter skills in particular, it's easiest to *teach* them to kids. Though it's equally easy to leave kids with a bad experience. So let's look at what it takes to teach and learn winter skills (and amaze people online with stories of "those crazy people up north").

"Sweat kills, you understand that? Never forget. Sweat kills." Yep, to say that mantra is ingrained in my memory is an understatement. Growing up in central North Dakota, I had plenty of opportunities to learn about the critical skills you need to survive the horrible, life-threatening winter conditions.

Oh, wait ... that's the socially correct way to describe winter in the northern United States. Let me rephrase my statement: Winters rocked growing up, and this is a chapter a) about how I learned to enjoy winters in the north, and b) that I hope will freak out as many southerners as possible.

For me growing up, the rule was (as I've mentioned previously): "Never get cold, never get hungry." Great rule. But to follow it, you need to have a few skills in your arsenal.

The first is understanding the skill of being prepared. Part of being prepared is practicing the skill of having the right stuff when you need it. Jumper cables are a great example. It's vital to have a set in your truck. Being prepared says that you have a good working battery in the truck, so the jumper cables are a backup, not a necessity.

It's just a normal day
up north.

Being prepared also means that you have the knowledge necessary to use the stuff you bring with you. Take clothing, for instance. I have the kids pack (don't do the packing for them!) a spare set of clothes whenever we're venturing out in the winter. That way, they always have a set of warm, dry clothes. As adults, it's our responsibility to teach kids how to dress in layers and stay dry, and to have the spare set as a safety feature.

The mistake many adults make is chewing kids out when they get wet. It's important for all of us to learn some of these lessons by getting a little cold in a safe environment—instead of getting angry. When kids get wet, it never hurts to keep it light and default to picking on them instead of blowing up at them.

STARTING A FIRE

This is a valuable skill that people are rarely taught anymore. But if you're going to spend any time in the outdoors, especially in the winter, you need to practice starting a fire. It's an easy skill to learn in the backyard with your kids in the summer. Then, when you're out in adverse conditions in the winter, you can work on starting a fire there as additional practice.

Remember when my dad challenged me to a fire-starting contest on the side of a mountain in the pouring rain (see Chapter 12)? He won with one match, and I learned how to start a fire in wet, cold conditions. When it comes to winter, though, the fuel is cold enough—and even if you don't know it, it's also wet, making it very difficult to use in starting a fire.

Taking the time during the winter to start fires with your kids, even when you don't need one, helps expand on this basic skill. Fires on the ice while you're ice fishing are also a lot of fun, and they provide the opportunity for kids to learn some basic cooking skills as well. Remember: Never get cold, never get hungry.

FIRST AID

We think about a lot of things when we head outside in the winter, but first aid is usually low on the list. Talk to a pessimist about all the things that could transpire on a winter day hunting in the hills; they're probably right. Put knives and gravity together and things happen.

Knowing the basic first aid for stopping bleeding, making splints, and treating common ailments is key to being prepared in the outdoors. Interesting observation to look for: The more you teach your kids about first aid, the more preventative actions they take—and remind *you* to take, as I have learned.

SITUATIONAL AWARENESS

Awareness is an important skill, one that is fun to teach in the outdoors. Play games and have the kids identify things they haven't noticed yet. When you find something they don't know or understand, look up the answers together so that you have a learning experience. Which weather patterns lead to other weather patterns is a great example.

Another key area to talk through with your kids is driving and vehicle operation. Kids need to know what's safe and what's not—on the road, around the vehicle, and in the vehicle. What can you hook onto to pull a car out of the ditch, for example, and where is it safe to stand?

Physics is important to understand, and situational awareness allows you to make wise decisions. It's only by pointing out and talking about *your* situational awareness that kids learn to have their *own* situational awareness.

THE BUDDY SYSTEM

It's a simple skill and a lot of fun to hit the outdoors with someone else. Everything in the outdoors is easier with two or more people.

When it comes to winter activities, a buddy is essential. All the skills we've talked about so far become even more helpful and effective if you're not by yourself.

Again, if you look at most outdoor tragedies, one of the common elements is someone who is out alone (see Chapter 12). But a second common denominator is a person who goes too far or stays out too long. So when you're spending time with your kids during winter outdoor activities, put them in the position of responsibility as your buddy. It will build their maturity and strengthen your relationship with them.

RESPECT

I'm sure most people will disagree with me on this one. But with nearly fifty years of living in the outdoors, I'm sticking to my guns. Besides: It isn't every day that a dyslexic guy like me takes the time to figure out that for respect to be a skill, it also has to be verb.

It's one thing to tell our kids that winter has cold temperatures; it's another to teach them how to *respect* those cold temperatures. All you need to do is tune in to any weather report to hear how we need to be afraid of all the scary cold temperatures and windy conditions. That's fear. What I'm talking about, though, are the actions we take that show we respect Mother Nature. The more skills we learn and the more knowledge we gain, the more things we can safely do in the outdoors during the winter. We need to teach our kids that the *action* of respect is what keeps us from going too far or staying out too long.

I guess when all is said and done, winter is scary if you try it in shorts and a T-shirt. But if you expand on the basic outdoor skills you need to stay comfortable and full, you can have a lot of fun in the winter. It's all about having a positive outdoor experience. To do that with your kids, you just need to learn these skills together and stretch yourselves a little bit at a time.

And when someone says you're nuts, just grin and say it's a normal day up north.

part three

DEMONSTRATING PRINCIPLES

Don't forget: They are learning from your example.

chapter 22

TAGGING ALONG

I was five years old when the Scout troop my dad helped lead embarked on a fifty-mile hike on the Lewis & Clark Trail. The plan was for two days of hiking with a day at the lake to finish it up.

I'm not sure whether I asked or if Dad just knew I wanted to go along, but at five I hiked all fifty miles. The funny part of the story is that I remember everyone cooking supper when I went into the tent to roll out my sleeping bag. When I was done, I came out and they were serving breakfast. Apparently, I took a long time to roll out a sleeping bag when I was five.

I am often asked what my wife and I have done that has made our kids know what they do at their age. The answer is pretty simple (though you should know that we haven't done the things we've done simultaneously!). You see, one of the things I learned from the way I was raised—something that has been reinforced as we've raised our own kids—is that there is no good replacement for doing things together as a family. The more your kids tag along, the more they learn. What they learn is up to you.

Young kids love their parents unconditionally and want to be just like them when they grow up. As parents, then, it is our responsibility to unconditionally love them back and set an example that they grow up to want to follow.

I won't go into any of the horror stories I witnessed growing up that involved adults who gave their kids plenty of lessons on what *not* to do—along with many bad memories. What I am going to do is talk about the principles I learned growing up that make tagging along an invaluable lifelong teaching experience for both adults and kids.

I knew more about cooking over an open fire before I was ten than most adults know about cooking at home. Dad's rule, as I've said, was: "Never get cold, never get hungry." It didn't matter what we were doing in the outdoors; we followed this rule.

It's amazing how, when things aren't going so well, getting warm and putting some food in your belly puts everything in perspective. When I take kids or new folks into the outdoors, I overprepare for staying warm and full. If you listen to kids especially, they will open up and be honest over a meal, giving you the chance to learn what makes them tick. Food opens the heart if you let it.

Kids learn integrity when the game warden comes; they watch you and emulate what you do. I love it when we get the opportunity to talk to the warden when the kids are with us. When you set an honest example, you get to be honest in front of your kids.

One time, after a hard day fishing on the river, we had loaded the boat and the local warden was checking folks at the dock. He asked the boys how we did, and they were sharing all sorts of stories of the day. Then the warden asked seven-year-old Peter what he thought of catching the brown trout. Peter got a concerned expression on his face and looked at me. His cartoon bubble said: "Dad, how does he know I caught a brown trout?" So I looked at him and said: "It's okay. Tell him about your trout."

Kids learn integrity when they see it in action.

On the way home, we talked about how integrity is being honest even when no one is around, and how you never have to worry about getting in trouble if you're honest. Kids learn respect and integrity when they see it in action.

One of the things I never gave enough credit to is how many safety practices kids learn when they tag along. I didn't realize it at the time, but when the kids were along, I not only told them the dos and don'ts, I explained the why as well. As a family, we did this everywhere we went.

The importance of explaining the why really became evident to me when my kids started politely correcting adults on all sorts of basic safety practices. I have to snicker with pride when we're at the gun range and I hear one of the kids tell someone that "there are no mistakes with guns, just bad decisions." Never get mad or annoyed at them or belittle them when your kids ask questions. What's important is that you take every question seriously and explain the why to the kid's ability level. That's how you build positive relationships.

One of the things our kids have learned by tagging along in the outdoors is respect and being polite. I'll admit: It wasn't our plan as parents to do this. But hey, stick with what works, right? As I said earlier, my wife and I have never spoken the phrase "use your inside voice." Really, to be honest, I still don't know what it means—and I'm an adult. Is there a decibel rating for inside voices posted somewhere?

What Kirsten and I did—and like I said, it was unplanned—was reference things the kids learned in the outdoors. As parents, we still laugh about the first time we were sitting in church and the boys were getting a little loud. I put my finger to my mouth and whispered: "Sssshhhh ... hunting voices." The kids spent the rest of the service competing to see who could be the quietest.

From then on, when we set an expectation for them, we gave them an outdoor example they had witnessed and practiced while tagging along. That way they knew what the expectation was and if they were meeting it. Kids really hurt when they get in trouble for something they didn't understand. Just because we as adults get it doesn't mean kids do. Learning outdoor skills is fun and applies to every area of life.

Tagging along needs to be fun, but it also needs to be a privilege. Kids need to earn the chance to come along, and we adults need to be fun enough for kids to want to come along. This requires two things. When kids are given a whole host of items that steal their creativity and their longing to explore, that's on us as the adults. Secondly, it's human nature to take risks and explore. Kids, especially boys, want to explore and learn. Make sure you let them tag along on trips so that they get to learn, take some chances, stretch themselves, and explore new places. They will beg to go again.

At the same time, we all need to learn that work comes first and the outdoors second. Live this example for your kids, hold them to it, and let them earn the chance to tag along.

I have overcome a lot in my life. Looking back on the many days I got to tag along with my dad in the outdoors, it's easy to see that most of what I learned growing up that has helped me through life, I learned on trips where I got to tag along with Dad. When I was learning how to walk again, for example, after getting burned as a volunteer firefighter, that fifty-mile hike of mine at five was always on my mind. If I could do it at five, why not thirty?

Let kids tag along and learn. They will love you for it.

The lessons from a hunt don't stop ...
even at the grill.

chapter 23

OUTDOOR PRINCIPLES

As I was falling very quickly from sixteen feet in the air, I clearly remember thinking about the words of wisdom my dad would impart on me when he saw me lying on the ground.

Now, I didn't *need* to hear anything from him. It should have been obvious by my falling sixteen feet holding a large dead tree branch in my hands that I had made a miscalculation. Yes, long before I hit the ground, I knew I should not have jumped from a healthy limb to a dead one to get more firewood to cook supper.

In the end, I landed on the side of the hill and rolled down with some bumps and bruises—and the knowledge that I shouldn't do that again. I don't know if Dad was ever aware of my acrobatics that day, but I'm pretty sure I know what he would have said if he'd witnessed what had happened.

Fast-forward a bunch of years, and we were having a large fish fry in our backyard. There were more than eighty people milling around in the space, and in the middle, we had a campfire for s'mores. Just as he was every other day, our five-year-old son Peter was nestled up to the fire with a burning stick in his hand. This was nothing new for him.

He knew how to start the fire with two matches and, more importantly, how to put it out cold to the touch by mixing and stirring.

At some point in the day, an older lady in the group had come to me pretty concerned, pointing out that Peter was playing in the fire. It was probably not my most diplomatic response, but I replied: "Well, if he gets burned, he won't do it again." I received an old lady huff, and the woman turned around and headed off to find a wiser, "real" adult.

Unfortunately for her, she found my dad.

Knowing that this older, wiser Olson would save Peter from the imminent campfire of death that would consume him in front of eighty people, the woman said: "Your grandson is playing in the campfire. He's going to get burned."

Without missing a beat, and with no thought whatsoever, Dad looked at her and said: "You can't get a diploma unless you pay the tuition."

Apparently, that wasn't the right answer either.

Those of you already telling someone how anti-safety I am, hear me out. I'm all about safety; that's why I'm anti-lots-of-facts-free-rules. (I'm pretty sure that isn't a real term, but I'm dyslexic so I'm allowed). There are rules that are important and necessary. But an overwhelming number of situations you encounter in the outdoors and in life are better confronted with *principles*, not *rules*. Here's the difference: Rules have hard and fast dos or don'ts. Principles are decision-making processes that help you not do something dumb, like jumping to a dead tree limb sixteen feet in the air.

There are seven of these principles that I learned growing up that have molded me into the person I am today. For those of you still concerned about Peter hurting himself: These principles kept *me* safe as well.

I'm going to go through them quickly here, but I'll cover each of them in depth in the chapters ahead.

JUST BECAUSE YOU KNOW DOESN'T MEAN THEY DO

We need to remember that our journey through life is different from everyone else's. It's easy to look at someone's actions and criticize those actions. Instead, ask: "Has anyone told them?" Then take the time to kindly help them.

LEARN, TEACH, UNDERSTAND

"I can do it myself" is a mindset that gets us all in trouble. Being open to wisdom from someone who has gone before you makes a lot of sense, not to mention the fact that it's cheaper and safer.

Taking the time to teach someone is also important for protecting those who are still learning from making tough or unsafe mistakes. The result is that you gain a better understanding of everything you've learned and taught.

LEAVE EVERY PLACE BETTER THAN YOU FOUND IT

Life comes with responsibility. Leaving every place better than we found it keeps the world cleaner. It also reminds us that we're responsible for the environments we interact with.

Carry things a little further and leave every *person* better than you found them and the world will be a better place.

ACT WITH DECISIVENESS

Look at most mistakes in the outdoors and you will find stories of indecisiveness. When hard situations present themselves and important decisions need to be made, have the insight to look at the big picture and the ability to see the effects of your actions before you proceed. When you've considered everything and it's time to act, decisiveness is imperative.

YOUR ACTIONS HAVE CONSEQUENCES

When we make a decision, we set into motion a series of events. Some decisions are seemingly insignificant while others are quite destructive. Knowing the consequences of your actions, before you take them, is the key to making wise decisions.

BE PREPARED

You don't need to be a Boy Scout to be prepared. Most people think that being prepared is all about carrying one of everything wherever you go. In reality, it's more of a mindset than a packing list.

BE KIND, NOT RIGHT

At the end of the day, there are lots of options out there for hunting, fishing, conservation, agriculture, and all the other stuff we do in the outdoors. There are also lots of effects that impact each group involved in any situation. Taking the time to be kind in all we do is more important than being right.

When it comes to these principles, I can honestly say that I learned them all in great detail in the outdoors thanks to the examples I observed growing up. I can also say that Dad was right when he once told me I'd learn more about the principles when I *didn't* use them to make decisions. Yep, paying tuition is necessary. Because we gain responsibility with experience, not rules or age.

My childhood fall marked the only time I've looked for firewood off the ground. And Peter never got burned because he had already learned that lesson. When we truly care about our kids and keeping them safe, we teach them principles and decision making. Don't forget: The definition of success is having a positive outdoor experience.

*Never pass up the chance to teach
someone else what you know.*

chapter 24

JUST BECAUSE
YOU KNOW

"OOOUCH!"—along with all sorts of other loud noises, accompanied by even more jumping around and lots of tears—was how our first sit for muleys went on a beautiful November day.

It was my son Dan's first time out hunting the badlands with me, and two things were very obvious. First, we were not going to see any deer in this spot. And second, I had foolishly assumed that my five-year-old knew that you should look for cactus before you sit down. Nothing says bonding like pulling thorns out of your kid's butt in the badlands on his first deer hunting trip.

This is when I started to understand the principle that "just because you know something doesn't mean they do." It's a principle that is frequently overlooked by us parents as we raise our kids. In fact, we all tend to overlook it when we assume that other people we meet share our same experiences. When was the last time you heard someone say: "They're adults, why don't they know that?"

One of the places where this phenomenon is most evident is in the anti-gun debate. Wrong assumptions are made possible by the misunderstanding that age equals maturity. The reality, though, is that maturity comes from learning responsibility through life's lessons. And these lessons can only come from life's experiences.

*It's better to be thorough
with directions than
sorry you didn't ask.*

The reason *I* knew I needed to look for cactus before I sat down in the badlands is that I kneeled on a cactus when I was about Dan's age and learned that painful lesson first-hand. Not to mention the fact that every couple of years, I forget the lesson and Mother Nature gives me a refresher course in cactus observance.

You might be thinking to yourself: This is a good rule of thumb for parents raising kids. But how and why is it a principle we need to teach our kids? Good question. Here's the answer: As adults, when we don't know this principle, we hurt our kids. In the badlands, for example, I forgot to warn Dan of his imminent pain in the butt—which is a funny story now and had no lasting consequences. But when we adults assume that kids know something that they don't, the consequences *can* be tragic.

Another ramification of not understanding this principle is the emotional damage caused when kids are punished for not knowing something we've never taught them. This also translates into anger and bitterness when we get upset with adults for not knowing what we know.

There are several reasons why this principle is an important one to teach kids in the outdoors. First, it's part of the how behind the "learn, teach, understand" principle I cover in the next chapter. Second, it helps us meet people where they are. It teaches us as parents how to evaluate our kids' skill sets and determine our kids' abilities and limitations. Finally, it's one of the most important safety principles that exists. That's why the consequences of not teaching and not using the principle can be so bad.

Many years ago, we were at an outdoor kids' event at the local refuge and the kids were sitting in a fire safety class. The instructor asked the kids what they needed to do if they wanted to have a campfire.

All the kids in the room excitedly raised their hands to take a shot at the answer. I shook my head as the instructor called on my son Peter—not because I was afraid of the answer Peter would give, but because I knew he had the right technical answer ... which wasn't the answer the instructor was looking for. The instructor was looking for "ask your parents." But seven-year-old Peter said: "You need to create a clear zone four times the height of your fire. Then you need to collect two handfuls of matchstick-size wood so that you can start the fire with two matches. When you're done with the fire, you need to put it out by mixing and stirring it so that it's cold to the touch." This is the right, safe, technical answer most adults in our country don't know.

When we start teaching our kids this principle when they're young, a few things naturally happen. First, as parents, we create the habit of asking questions of our kids instead of unknowingly judging them. In turn, our kids learn that it's okay to ask questions and to speak up when they don't know something. As the parent of four kids myself, I forget who I've taught what to most days.

Teaching this principle early on also helps you and your kids learn how to safely communicate with each other. This leads to strong relationships with your kids as they grow older. It's not a guarantee, but I don't know many parents who teach and follow this principle who don't have healthy relationships with their teenagers—skipping out on the drama. When someone is raised with this principle in the outdoors, they naturally teach it to others—including their own kids as they grow up.

Living and demonstrating principles is the foundation to teaching principles. Take, for example, learning how to net fish. As my kids were growing up, I demonstrated and at the same time talked through how I was netting each fish. As they got older and as they were able, I had the kids do the netting and explain what they were doing both to me and to the younger siblings in the boat.

It's also important to give kids opportunities to watch you teaching principles to others, and to let them teach the principles as well. Earlier (see Chapter 20), I talked about the day Peter shot his first buck with a bow. You'll remember that he was in the tree stand with his uncle, who had never hunted before. Peter had the chance to explain to his uncle what he was doing and why. I still couldn't tell you which one of them was shaking more when they got out of the tree. I was close enough in the next tree stand that I could stop anything I needed to while giving Peter the room he needed to learn and teach.

We all need the chance to fail as we learn, and this is also true when we're teaching principles. Don't prevent your kids from having opportunities to safely fail. It may be a cactus in the butt, knocking a limit of fish off the line during failed netting attempts, or getting a little cold because they forgot to remember their rain gear. Learning little lessons early in life teaches kids the principles, and the ramifications of following and not following become clearer to them later in life.

When you understand the idea that just because you know something doesn't mean the next person does, you build trusting relationships with your kids, you give them an important safety mindset, and you help them meet other people where they are without condemnation. All thanks to a simple concept that most people overlook or misunderstand.

Embrace the satisfaction of teaching and learning.

chapter 25

LEARN, TEACH, UNDERSTAND

It's hard to believe that it's been more than a decade since my sons Dan and Peter said they wanted to make fishing tackle to earn money for ammunition at the range. The boys were ten and eight years old, respectively, at the time. A couple of years back as part of a school project, Peter was asked to put in his own words how he would explain how he was taught at home and what was important about it. Here's what he wrote:

> There are a lot of ways to learn how to go out and catch fish, but I can't tell you how much I appreciate it when someone takes the time to share what they know with me. In turn, there is a joy in teaching others what you have learned on the water. Not to mention, when we take the time to teach others to fish, we are not only helping them learn to be better anglers, but we understand fishing better ourselves. It's really simple: learn, teach, understand, and leave ripples.

As adults, we need to step back and let this soak in for a little bit. Kids learn from us whether we think we're teaching them or not. Look back on your own story: What did *you* learn growing up? How many of those lessons are helpful? How many are negative? How many don't matter all these years later?

I can tell you that the people who have invested time in me are the reason I've been able to achieve what I have and survive some pretty sticky situations. I was taught, and learned, many of their life lessons in the outdoors.

*Sometimes the best way
to teach something is
to just do it.*

I was listening to a podcast the other day that talked about how people miss out on the opportunity to learn when they're fishing because they look for crowds and then fish in those areas. The podcaster was right. The reason people don't take the risk to venture out on their own is that many of them have never had anyone teach them the basics. Most kids today are taught to avoid all risks, and to try only if they know they're going to succeed.

Another thing to understand is that many kids simply don't have the opportunities a lot of us grew up with. I recently heard, for example, about a high school football coach in a rural community who had more than thirty players. None of them had two parents, and a few had no parents at home at all.

Without getting into specifics about my age: I just picked up my first pair of bifocals so that I can tie leaders to fish with. Yet I am still learning all sorts of lessons in the outdoors. Many of these lessons emerge as I *teach* my kids about life in the outdoors.

I learned a lot of stuff about the outdoors from my dad growing up, but there were plenty of things he didn't know. That's where others stepped in and taught me what *they* knew—some of it good information, some of it not so accurate! Case in point: I've tried to get the hang of goose hunting since junior high. I keep threatening to write a book called *Confessions of a Failed Waterfowler*. But a friend pointed out that I'm just a conservationist—you know, catch-and-release goose hunting!

A few years ago, I met some local guys who said they'd help me put some geese on the ground. Since then, I've learned that everything I was taught about goose hunting growing up was wrong. By simply getting some accurate information and building our skill sets, we've had a lot of fun goose hunting the last few years. It doesn't matter how

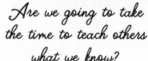

Are we going to take the time to teach others what we know?

old we are, we all need someone to learn from and some-one to teach.

When it comes right down to it, there are a couple of questions we adults need to ask ourselves. First, are we going to take the time to teach others what we know? It seems like a simple enough question to answer. But it can be a little more complex when you sit down and think it over. Maybe the better question, then, is: What do I know? I didn't understand how much I *didn't* know until I started trying to teach my kids about waterfowl hunting. I needed someone to teach all of us.

For the last several years, my sons Peter and Andrew have traveled to Minnesota to fish the Student Angler Tournament

Trail. As a parent, I can't express how valuable their time with Captain Todd has been in helping them grow up to be the young men they are today. We all need people to learn from who aren't our parents. For me, there were three guys who took me hunting, fishing, and camping and reinforced the lessons I was learning about the outdoors and life from my own dad.

As I said earlier, nowadays there are lots of kids without parents. And there are even more *parents* who are longing for someone to help them learn about the outdoors and life. Too many parents and people stress out about this fact.

Let me simplify it for you: All you need to do is do what you know and love doing, with someone else. You don't need a degree in education. You just need to share your passion with people who are willing to learn. The key word here is *willing*. Most of us learn best through example and by asking questions. So all we have to do is share what we know with those who want to know it.

We also need to know that it's okay to ask for help; it's okay to ask someone to teach us. If they say no, don't feel rejected. Just keep looking for someone who's worth learning from.

I love the outdoors. I love spending time with my family, teaching and learning in the outdoors. I am the son, father, friend, employee, and director I am because of the lessons I've learned in the outdoors, none of which would have been possible without embracing the principle of "learn, teach, understand."

I'm excited about the future, knowing that I'm passing it on to my kids in the outdoors.

The aftermath of the 2011 flood
in Minot, North Dakota.

chapter 26

LEAVE EVERY PLACE BETTER THAN YOU FOUND IT

Raising kids in the outdoors is a lot of fun, and it's really only as hard as you make it. But you have to be willing to do one thing: live it.

This is especially true when it comes to teaching the principle I'm covering here. I learned the concept of "leave every place better than you found it" long before I was required to know it as the essence of the Boy Scouts' Outdoor Code. The real power of this principle, though, goes well beyond what many people think. That's why it's treated by most parents as nothing more than the "clean your room" rule.

A couple of years back, I was asked at a public forum about when parents should start teaching fire safety to their kids. My response—"when they're born"—caught people off guard. "Hold on, Geremy. Are you crazy?" was their cartoon bubble. It might well be yours, too, as you're reading this ... if those words didn't actually come out of your mouth, that is.

Let me explain, just as I did to the audience members that day.

Your kids are observing you from the day they're born. They will mimic your actions and words. For you new parents out there, understanding—and accepting—this truth early on makes life as a parent much easier.

Talk to any parent who has older children and you'll hear stories good and bad about the kids mimicking their parents. Kids don't have understanding in their early years. So as they're growing up, we need to give them the why behind what we do. And we need to do it in a way that allows them to learn at their own pace in a safe environment (physical and emotional).

You never know how your selfish actions are going to affect people.

I can't remember a time growing up when, as a family, we didn't look for something to pick up before we left a place. It was the example I saw time and time again. Go camping, clean up your area and more.

It isn't always easy or convenient. I'll never forget the first time I thought to myself as a parent: *"I'm tired, it's late, the boys are crabby, let's just go home."* I would soon come to realize just how important the principle of "leave every place better than you found it" really is. Looking back on that night now, I realize how foundational the decision I ended up making has been to the maturity of my kids today.

"Leave every place better than you found it" is one of the simplest principles to teach and model. But what I realized that night by a small Minnesota river is that it's also one of the principles that is easiest to get complacent about—which *itself* is a lesson I would have been teaching my kids had I decided to go home without practicing "leave every place better than you found it"! The lesson they would have learned in that scenario would have been: "You can change the rule based on your feelings or situation." Not a good lesson.

So that night, we cleaned up our own stuff and others' garbage as well. It wasn't a happy time. But it served as a memorable lesson for both the boys and me. I know they don't remember the experience, but it was crucial to their upbringing.

In fact, its importance would become better illuminated years later, during a trip to the local gun range with the boys. As we pulled up, one of them announced: "What a mess."

"Yeah, it is," I replied.

As we set up that day, I talked about respect, responsibility, and integrity. At the end of our range time, we filled the site's garbage cans with the abundance of trash we had picked up. It was then that I witnessed the impact of that hard night we'd had at the river years before—because it was the boys, not me, who decided when the range area was clean enough for us to go.

The "leave every place better than you found it" principle is simple but essential for both outdoor conservation and for life. It teaches us that regardless of others' actions, we still need to do what's right. If we can't do that with a little garbage by the side of a lake, how are we supposed to do it when we're confronted with bigger challenges and temptations in life?

In 2011, the community I grew up in was devastated by flooding. It was so severe that most homes were well out of the identified flood zone, making them ineligible for flood insurance. Lots of heartache and devastation. As a family, we took the opportunity to help those in need. The same boys who chose to clean up the gun range took that same principle of "leave every place better than you found it" with them into the stench of the flood zone. I lost count of how many houses we helped clean that year, but I know the snow was falling when the last place was finished.

None of us wants a disaster to happen. But we live in a world with troubles. As parents, we need to use these times with our kids, not shelter them from them. During the floods, our boys witnessed firsthand the power of Mother Nature. They learned that no matter how much we may try to control her, we are not in charge. She is.

They also learned that the natural extension of "leave every place better than you found it" is "leave everyone better than you found them."

Let that sink in for a while. This principle is much tougher to teach and model. Right now, if you're human, you can probably pick out all the people who *don't* deserve to be treated better more easily than you could put in the extra effort to leave other people better than you found them. Yes, if we started with "leave everyone better than you found them," we'd have a hard time pulling it off, even as adults.

But it's easier to see hope for the world when we teach principles in the outdoors. Principles are more objective outside. They're easier to understand, for kids and adults alike. And they bring clarity and perspective whenever we deal with the inevitable difficulties of life. This was evident in every one of those flooded houses, and in all the decisions the boys have made since.

So if you're still wondering: Yes, staying a little longer with cranky toddlers to clean up some trash is worth it. Very worth it.

Teach the value of appropriate, measured action.

ACT WITH DECISIVENESS

I'm the proud dad of … a kind-of lifeguard at our local pool. What?

Well, my daughter Morgan doesn't turn fifteen until after this book hits the shelves. So she can only work the front desk until she reaches that magic number.

Yes, there are rules and regulations we live with in public places, but that's not the case in the outdoors. There, we have only the laws of nature. These laws are true whether we like them or not, and they don't change based on age or certifications.

That's why the outdoor principle of "act with decisiveness" is so very important to understand—and to live out right in front of your kids so that they can learn from your positive example.

This chapter isn't about fear, doom, and gloom. It's about perspective, and teaching the value of appropriate, measured action.

One summer, while she was getting off her boat, a gal fell off the dock and into water over her head. It was a miserable, rainy day, and she had a lot of clothes on.

A guy on the dock took action and kept her safe as best he could with a lot of boats loading around them in the rain. Another person ran down and helped the woman get safely to solid ground. That second person passed by multiple people who were watching everything play out. Those bystanders didn't know what was going on or what to do. It was the two people who acted with decisiveness who kept the woman from getting hurt worse than her pride did that day.

It's easy for us as adults to classify outdoor activities according to different levels of safety. Typically, the safest activities on our lists are the ones we're most familiar with. Conversely, the activities we classify as anything from more dangerous to most dangerous are the ones we're less familiar with. What's more dangerous? Rock climbing or shooting, water skiing or downhill skiing, a bonfire or a propane grill? The reality is that more people are killed in fishing accidents than in hunting accidents. And car accidents are more common than both.

What I'm getting at is that life in the outdoors is dangerous regardless of the activity or our comfort level with that activity. Mother Nature also doesn't care who a person is, how they live their life, or who they're related to. She has no feelings, and she doesn't care about ours. That's why it's vital to explain to our kids the causes and effects of our actions when we're in the outdoors. Like many things in life, one honest, simple, but bad decision in the outdoors can lead to injury or death. This is equally true whether we hesitate or we quickly have to figure out what's going on around us because immediate action is required. When it comes down to it, hesitation can be just as dangerous as, or even worse than, a bad decision.

As the dad of a future lifeguard, the question I'm asking myself isn't "what should I teach her?" It's "what have I taught her?" Morgan has all the lessons and skills she's learned in the outdoors that will enable her to apply the principle of "act with decisiveness," just as the guy on the dock did with the gal who fell into the water.

The skills we learn in the outdoors are easily applied to everyday life.

The first skill is situational awareness. As we raise our kids in the outdoors, it's critical to have them practice this skill. It can be a lot of fun if you simply ask your kids lots of questions. What bird is that? Where's the boat ramp? What color was that truck? What's the speed limit? Where's camp from here? How far away is the storm? When you're consistent enough in asking fun questions, your kids will catch on and start asking them of you before you can ask them yourself! Over time, the kids will even start catching you not paying attention to your surroundings. Thank and praise them when this happens; it's the time you know that they get it.

The next important skill is understanding cause and effect. If I stay out in the lightning storm, then what? A couple of years ago, our son Peter was out on the water fishing a tournament when he got a shock from a thunderstorm off in the distance. He turned to the boat captain and said: "We are going to shore *NOW!*" They wouldn't have made it back to the ramp, he says today, if they had tried to race the storm back. Peter is now an unpaid meteorologist on the water. I have no worries of being caught off guard by a storm when he's with me.

This is where our comfort in outdoor activities gets us in trouble. The more comfortable we are with an activity, the more likely we are to become complacent about the power of that activity. In other words, we don't respect the effects of Mother Nature.

Regardless of whether Morgan is a lifeguard or out hunting in the badlands, she will be confronted with situations that require decisiveness anchored in the awareness she has in that moment. In these scenarios, both her life and the lives she has committed to watch over will be on the table.

Hesitation and uncertain actions leave you in danger for a longer time. Decisive action made with situational awareness and a solid understanding of the causes and effects of your surroundings reduces exposure to bad outcomes. When it comes right down to it in the outdoors, decisive actions keep us safer and allow us to help and save others.

As parents, we need to live out principles like this one and consistently teach our kids the practical information they need to make wise decisions. That way they'll have the skills to use and the principles to apply when they're faced with the time to act.

They won't always get it right, just like us. So don't scold them for acting or not acting. Work with them on how to act more effectively.

Whether Morgan is a fifteen-year-old lifeguard or just swimming at the lake before that magic date on the calendar, she will know what to do if she's faced with a crisis. More importantly, she will do it decisively so that the outcome is positive.

Maybe it's just me,
but I think something went very wrong.

YOUR ACTIONS HAVE CONSEQUENCES

Have you ever opened a bait bucket you thought was empty, only to find out that you have a compelling gag reflex?

While you're avoiding this question by bringing up someone else's oversight, I'll just point out that I'm sure no one else has neglected some much-needed maintenance on a boat or vehicle that may have led to a shorter or longer trip than anticipated.

The principle of "actions have consequences" is usually chalked up as just another fact of life—which is true. But it's also an important outdoor principle that we need to teach our kids.

The obvious place to start is gun safety. Every action we take with a firearm can have immediate and final consequences. So it's easy for people to overcompensate for this principle when they're dealing with guns. You can just plain forget the value of teaching the principle in *every* area of life. When you think about it, there is a cause and effect—sometimes good, sometimes bad—for absolutely everything we do. It's essential to teach our kids the implications of their actions, both in life at home and in the outdoors.

I'm probably going to cover this backwards for many of you, but hey: I'm dyslexic, so I'm allowed. The result of teaching our kids the concept of cause and effect in the outdoors is that they have practical, tangible experiences they can easily relate to their daily life. When our son Dan was in fifth-grade basketball, for example, he couldn't pass to save his life. His coach thought about it, then told him to pass the ball just like the follow-through he used when he was hunting birds. Ding ding ding: He started making every pass. Even though Dan didn't understand the physics at the time, he did understand the cause and effect of swinging with the bird to make a shot. The same concept held on the basketball court, and vice versa.

When we're teaching our kids that all actions have consequences, we need to let them experience and live with some of those consequences. I guarantee you, for instance, that my daughter remembers her sunscreen now after her first—and so far only—post-sunburn, uncontrollable itching experience.

For me, this principle became incredibly clear during a camping trip in high school. We didn't gather enough firewood to cook chicken, and it was obvious that we needed to get more or we would get salmonella. So I looked around and found some easy-to-get wood that was close. Remember that sixteen-foot drop of mine out of the tree (see Chapter 23)? When that dead limb was breaking, I recall thinking: "If this doesn't kill me, it's really going to hurt." Well, I lived through that learning experience and promptly put it on my "don't do that again" list.

We've all tried things that were dumb and a little more dangerous than we should have tried. Our kids will too. That's why it's vital to offer them an emotionally safe environment that allows them to learn the cause-and-effect concept.

You may be asking: "What do you mean by that?" As parents, we naturally overreact or get angry when we're caught off guard by something our kids try. This hurts our relationships with them and teaches them a sort of warped version of the idea that actions have consequences. It's as though exploring equals angry parents, making mistakes equals disappointed parents, asking questions equals annoyed parents, etc. In other words, *everything* we do as parents is an example of this principle. Thus, if you have a negative reaction, it's a negative experience for your kids. But if you choose to have a positive reaction, then it's a positive experience. We need to be aware of this phenomenon and act accordingly.

When we take the time to purposely teach our kids cause and effect in an emotionally safe environment, we build our relationships with them and set ourselves up for lots of fun if we let it happen. Unfortunately, many parents do everything they can to, for instance, keep their kids from getting a fishhook stuck in themselves or someone else when they're learning how to fish. These parents focus solely on the negative.

In contrast, when my wife, Kirsten, and I taught our own kids how to cast, we focused on helping them to always be aware of their rod tip and lure. When there was a miscast (and there were many!), the kids were simply met with a humorous comment or a question that reinforced the point without anger or admonishment. And when the inevitable time came and the kids got stuck with a hook, we used it as a learning experience and made a video.

This mindset promotes the relationship you need to cultivate with your kids so you can have the more-serious conversations about cause and effect with them. Adults put a lot of time into talking about the dangers of guns, for example. But each year, more people are injured in or die from accidents in the outdoors than from guns. It's equally important to teach our kids how to safely pull someone out of the ditch with a tow strap, drive on a two-track road, dress in layers, or judge ice conditions. So find ways for you and your kids to see the positive and negative consequences of actions; just as you might do at the gun range with a watermelon, for example.

Another great resource for parents are news stories about outdoor tragedies. Talk with your kids about what went wrong in these incidents, what it would have taken to avoid the negative result, and how they themselves can make sure they won't end up in the same place. The key here as a parent is to not mock or belittle the people in the story. Doing so only teaches our kids to be judgmental, and if they ever end up in the same situation, you've already negatively judged them. So instead, look at the facts and keep the conversation constructive.

Finally, every year I have the chance to accompany my sons to a couple of events called Men In Boats and Men On Ice. This last summer, Andrew and I hit the water with Gary at Men In Boats. Andrew had originally wanted to stay home to watch a demolition derby but had decided to come with me instead. He ended up having the chance to help Gary catch his first limit of fish on that lake. He experienced as well the joy that comes from helping someone else.

YOUR ACTIONS HAVE CONSEQUENCES

As parents, it's important for us to understand the balance in teaching this principle because there are also positive consequences to our actions. When you think about it, generally in life, there are more positive actions that have positive consequences than negative ones.

When we build a strong relationship with our kids, we can ingrain in them the principle of "your actions have consequences." Or maybe it's when we teach our kids this principle in a safe environment that we build a strong relationship with them!

Either way, skip all the anger and judgment toward your kids and instead start having fun learning cause and effect with them. Keep the serious stuff serious and enjoy the rest together. Your kids will love you for it.

And that will be a positive consequence.

Every kid and every situation is different...
very different.

BE PREPARED

It was a snowy December night in North Dakota. In fact, it was bad enough outside that church ended early to ensure that everyone could get home safely. I vividly remember Dad asking people to call him when they got home so that he'd be sure no one was stranded on their journey. Some of the members had a forty-mile drive ahead of them.

I was fifteen years old, and I was done with everything I was responsible for. So I turned to Dad and said goodbye.

That's when the question was asked: "Where's he going?"

"Ice fishing," Dad replied.

The question then grew into a discussion. The fifty-plus-year-old guy that Dad was making sure made it home safely wanted to know why I was going ice fishing in a snowstorm while he was being rushed to his house.

I don't know how Dad's answer impacted the concerned gentleman that night, but I do know how it impacted me. Dad looked the guy in the eye and said assuredly: "I know he has what he needs to survive any storm."

I drove to my favorite lake that night with all the confidence in the world, knowing I had proven to my dad that I understood what it fully means to "be prepared."

For many people, "Be Prepared" is the Boy Scout Motto. The phrase is often spoken as a jab at the person who brings everything including the kitchen sink when they go somewhere. But there's a lot more to this principle than we tend to realize. For starters, most people don't understand that "be prepared" is a principle as well as a skill. In my experience, the vast majority of people think that "be prepared" means bringing one of everything everywhere you go.

Well, simply put, that's wrong.

As parents, we have all sorts of choices to make. Many of these choices involve how we raise our kids. I don't have any empirical data to back up my assumption, but when it comes to raising kids, I will wager that most parents weigh their decisions on one thing: keeping the kids safe. In many cases, this leads to keeping kids *from* something: not letting them play with a burning stick in a fire; not letting them touch or see a gun; making them wear a life jacket on the dock, even when you're there—just to name a few.

As you think about these examples or about similar decisions *you* have made, remember that every kid and every situation is different. With that in mind, please keep the comments that follow in context.

Regardless of how much we want to keep our kids safe, we can't. There are countless circumstances and situations that are simply out of our control. That's why it's important to start teaching our kids at an early age how to identify what's going on around them and take appropriate action. The harsh reality of life is that the more you prevent your kids from decision making, the more danger they'll be in as they go through that life.

This is where, and why, teaching kids the principle of "be prepared" is so important. It's the foundation of the decision-making process, in the outdoors and practically everywhere else.

For me, it started with a Band-Aid.

When I was four or five, I got a handful of wallets, losing each of them out in the pasture chasing mice and coons. But I digress. The first thing Dad gave me for my wallet was a pair of Band-Aids.

"Always have a couple of Band-Aids wherever you go," he told me. "That way, if anyone gets a cut, you're prepared to do basic first aid."

As I grew up, Dad always asked *me* if I had a Band-Aid when someone needed one—instead of simply using his own. This subtle gesture only reinforced my basic understanding of the "be prepared" principle.

The other way we kids learned the principle while we were growing up was through "what if" questions. I think it's fair to say that it was almost a game. Dad would ask questions like:

- "What would you do if your paddle broke out on the water?"

- "What if you needed to keep food cold and you didn't have a cooler?"

- "How would you help a person with a broken leg on this trail?"

- "Do you have what you need if you had to spend the night outside when you weren't planning to?"

As you read through these questions yourself, you may see that they all have three-part answers. The first part is having the right stuff to do what you need to do; pretty straightforward. The next two, however, are aspects of being prepared that are usually overlooked:

- Do you have the knowledge base you need to make the decisions you'll face in each situation you encounter?
- Do you have the appropriate skill set to act on the decisions you make?

Let's get back to the Band-Aid. When Dad asked me if I had one in my wallet, he was also showing me when and how to use that Band-Aid. As I've said before (more than once!): Responsibility comes with experience, not age. As parents, the more we expose our kids to real-life situations in as controlled an environment as possible, the safer they will be as opposed to keeping them sheltered from those same situations. We teach our kids to swim, for example, a little bit at a time. Some pick it up faster, some slower. Isolating kids from danger their whole lives is like throwing them into the deep end of the pool with no training. It *may* work; but it usually doesn't.

What most parents have never been taught is that it's also important for us to teach our kids what to do when things don't go right in life. Being prepared, then, is also about having the fortitude to keep a cool head when things don't go according to plan.

One day when we were fishing at the dock with the boys, three-year-old son Peter backed up off the dock and slowly started sinking in the water with his eyes wide open. I'm convinced I still have hearing damage from the lady on the other end of the dock who screamed in uncontrollable panic. But I just calmly reached down, grabbed Peter's hand, and pulled him out. I gave him a hug and asked if he was all right. As he nodded, I told him: "Remember, you know how to swim." Then he nodded again as I added: "Next time you fall in the water, stay calm and swim to the dock." Getting mad at him for falling in would have only scared him. By staying calm instead, and explaining to him what to do, I helped him learn what it means to truly be prepared.

What's crucial to remember as we're raising our kids in the outdoors is that teaching them to be prepared is a process. And it's a process that is different for every family, every kid, and every activity. What's the same in each case is that we need to teach kids *all* the aspects of this principle—the knowledge, the skills, and the stuff they need to be prepared for whatever they face, especially when we aren't there to protect them and the unexpected happens.

Teaching kids to be prepared is the most vital principle you can instill in them to keep them safe.

Facts lead to knowledge
and knowledge leads to success.

KNOWLEDGE MEANS SUCCESS

We were all kids once, so we've all heard some of the same bad information from adults. Now that *we* are the adults, we need to break the pattern of bad advice and start teaching our kids how to think critically—and do so with facts. Not so our kids can be right; so they can be successful.

It doesn't matter whether you're a kid or an adult, facts lead to knowledge and knowledge leads to success. So when it comes to raising kids in the outdoors, knowledge is one of the keys not only to success, but also to helping kids keep the outdoors as a part of their lives once they've grown up.

When my oldest son, Dan, was in the middle of his freshman year of college, he was one of the guinea pigs for the principles and concepts in this book. Dan is the kid I made the most mistakes on and learned the most from.

In an interview with the Fish Stories website (FishStories. org) that year, Dan was asked who his favorite fishing trip had been with. His answer was one that would make any dad proud, and it undoubtedly grew out of the principles we've been talking about here. In the interview, Dan said that his favorite fishing trip wasn't with any one person in the past but, rather, when he gets to fish with the residents of Teen Challenge (a faith-based addiction treatment center) and teach them how to fish so that they have something to look forward to when they complete the program.

The lessons we learn with our kids at home, in the field, and on the water are full of the knowledge that leads to success in the outdoors and in life.

Reading is a tough topic for a dyslexic guy to cover, but as much as it pains me to say it ... reading is the foundation of knowledge. Teaching our kids how to read was the realm of my wife, Kirsten, for no other reason than the fact that she *could* read. My job, on the other hand, was to teach the kids how to discern and apply what they had read.

When it comes to reading and the outdoors, our favorite tool to this day is *The Hunting & Fishing Library* series produced by Dick Sternberg and Bill Lindner. With the exception of the archery volume, all the information in this series is practical, easy to read, and easy to use on the water or in the field (thanks to all the illustrations and pictures).

The strength of this series of books is what you should look for in any publication: facts, history, and experience, all in one package. If you read a single chapter in any of these books, you'll be more successful thanks to the knowledge you've gained. They're simple enough for young readers, too.

After forty-some years, I am still learning from these books. You can find them online, especially on used-book websites. Look for the ones that have the most balance. That way, you can read them with your kids and help them apply what they've discovered.

Two of the biggest roadblocks preventing kids from gaining knowledge are the phrases "just because" and "when you're older." Kids ask questions because they're learning. When they get responses like "just because" or "when you're older," they think you're telling them *not* to learn.

We need to meet kids where they are and help them learn. When they ask questions, they don't need all the details all at once. They just need enough to keep learning and gaining knowledge.

So whether you're in the outdoors or on the couch, take time to talk through kids' questions to their satisfaction. It's more important than I can express, especially when you consider the key side benefit: Your kids will communicate with you for life.

Once you've read about the outdoors with your kids, it's time to go make some mistakes—I mean, try out what you've learned. Application is part of knowledge, and mistakes are part of application. The principle goes like this: The key to success is failure, the goal is to not repeat your failures. It's rare to do something right the first time. We all get lucky once in a while, but usually we need to repeat things to get them right.

Knowledge also comes from experience, and experience comes from doing. So to gain knowledge, we have to try and fail until we succeed. Then we need to learn why we succeeded. And then we need to share why we succeeded with others. By being part of this process and observing it, our kids learn how to gain experience in a healthy way.

Teaching or sharing what we've learned is the only way we truly understand what knowledge we have. And as parents and adults, we need to give kids the chance to teach others what *they* have learned too. In fact, it's amazing what we *all* learn when we let kids learn.

*We all learn when
we let kids learn.*

Many years ago, my sons Dan and Peter and I were out ice fishing and were having no luck at all. Both boys were begging to use the flasher, but I kept saying it was too complicated for them. I went out to check our tip-up spread and started to hear hooting and hollering in the ice house, with cries of "I got one!" and "me too!" When I got back in the house, I found Dan teaching Peter how to play keep-away with the walleyes using the flasher.

It was the first—though certainly not the last—time I learned from my kids what I had taught them. They were playing keep-away until the fish bit or left. Every fish they ended up catching came six to ten feet off bottom before it bit. I learned a lot that night about walleyes, parenting, and knowledge because I watched Dan teach Peter what I had taught him—instead of getting mad because they had used the flasher.

Dan captured the definition of success in his Fish Stories interview. It's not about limits and bigger sizes. It's about learning, teaching others, and having a positive outdoor experience.

The foundation of this success is gaining knowledge and learning *together*. The lessons we learn together are the lessons that bring us success—in the outdoors and in life.

Take the time to care for and teach others
instead of boosting your own pride.

BE KIND,
NOT RIGHT

As a fishing tournament director, I have plenty of opportunities to, let's say, spell out the rules for anglers. As a parent, I have the same types of opportunities to impart the "right way" of doing things onto my kids. If you take a minute to think about it, you will pretty quickly come up with the areas in your life where you "have to" correct people for what they're doing wrong.

We are also living in a difficult time when most folks are perfectly fine determining what they think is right and wrong for themselves.

On one occasion, I was asked by an angler how I would handle another angler's actions that he deemed to be illegal. Just as I was about to answer, I paused, then asked for some time to think it over. It was obvious that the angler I was talking to was annoyed that I wasn't going to answer his question right away. But I paused because I was in the midst of working on how to write about the principle of being kind vs. right, and frankly I was a little stumped. This was the opportunity I needed to walk through the application of the principle in a real-world situation.

Asking the question "how can I be kind in this situation?" often leads to still more questions: What are both sides of the situation? What do they know? How much experience do they have, and what are those experiences? Am I being fair? Are they breaking a rule/law or my own preference? The list is almost endless.

In North Dakota, we have new rules about aquatic nuisance species. As is the case when any new rule is implemented, it's taking some people a bit of time to get adjusted to changing their behavior so that they are in compliance. Some of the rules have been deemed a little excessive, but at the end of the day they are still the rules.

Last summer, we saw two anglers almost get into a fistfight over someone leaving water in the live well of their boat just to go to the fish cleaning station that's at almost every boat ramp on the Missouri River system. When it comes to fish cleaning stations, it's interesting when you have people from three or four different states—with three or four different sets of rules—talking about how you need to clean your fish legally. I've seen scenarios like these turn into quite heated discussions over who's right.

What's interesting is what happens when we're confronted with situations like these and we step back and ask the questions we just talked about. "So, where are you from, and what are the rules there?" Take the time to listen and then say: "Hey, let's take a look at the rules here in this state and pull out the fishing regulations." Sometimes we learn we're doing something wrong, and other times we get the opportunity to teach somebody something new. But in either case, taking the time to handle the situation with kindness leads to anglers learning together instead of getting into unnecessary conflicts with each other.

My boys and I were working a booth at a sport show in North Dakota a few years back, and we naturally started talking fishing with the folks in the adjacent booths. On the second day of the show, one of the guys in the booth next to us, who was from out of state, asked to see some fish pics. The boys pulled out my phone and started showing him all the fish they'd caught that year on the Missouri River. I had to step in, though, when the man started lecturing the boys on their supposed lack of ethics, as evidenced by all the fish they were keeping. The man looked at me and said: "You're the reason there's no fish."

What are your motives?

After I calmed him down, we had a good conversation.

It would have been just as easy for me to chew this guy out for his actions. It also would have been just as easy to write him off as a jerk who hassled a couple of junior high kids for enjoying the outdoors and living off the land. I mean, really: How does his attitude get more kids into the outdoors? Instead, though, we discussed how each water system has different fish populations and natural sizes. In the Missouri River, for example, we have big fish that other natural lakes don't have. The man and I also talked about how it's critical to understand where people are coming from before making any judgments.

Because we took the time to be kind with one another, things ended well. If we had both doubled down on being right, it might well have been a different story.

Some of my favorite conversations in the boat are with a good friend of mine who didn't grow up in the outdoors. He routinely asks a powerful question that we should all keep in mind:

"So, what are the unwritten rules
for what we're doing today?"

Just think about it. What's the etiquette you grew up with for the boat ramps in your area? Boat ramp etiquette on the river is different than on the big water, which in turn is different than on a small lake. Ask yourself this question: "Am I holding someone accountable for an unwritten rule?"

Getting back to that question from the angler about whether someone else was doing something illegal or not ... I now realize that there's a more important question: "What are your motives in asking?" Maybe the better way to say it is: "What are my motives when I want to point out that somebody's wrong?"

We all have a choice: We can choose to be right, or we can choose to be kind. Choosing to be kind doesn't mean that we don't point out what somebody has done wrong or how they could do something better. But it does change how we interact with the people around us. It changes the motives behind our actions. And it changes our expectations of the outcome, too.

When we choose to be kind, we naturally meet people where they are. We also take a look at ourselves and where we've come from. Taking the "be kind" approach in more situations means there's rarely any conflict to defuse, because most people are looking for friends and guidance, and they understand they have a lot to learn in life. Taking the time to be kind means we're taking the time to care for and teach others instead of boosting our own pride. That's true regardless of what position of authority we're in, especially when it comes to the relationships we have with the people around us.

When you take the time to be kind instead of right, you help people grow. Including yourself.

Choosing between fear and ignorance ...
is still making a bad choice.

WISDOM, NOT FEAR

There's a lot of fear in our world right now. The 2020 pandemic was just the tipping point that stopped everything long enough for us to take a good, hard look at how afraid many people are. In fact, I had a magazine article on the agenda for December 2020 that I ultimately chose to write several months sooner than planned—i.e., when the pandemic struck—because its topic dominated virtually everyone's life when the pandemic hit.

As you read this chapter, take some detailed notes about what you're afraid of and why. It's okay to be honest because everyone is afraid sometimes. What matters is how we deal with our fears. And remember, too, that when it comes to our kids, they will learn how to confront their fears by *our* example.

We've all seen adults chewing out a kid for playing in a campfire. We've all suffered through long discussions about how old a kid should be to carry a gun in the outdoors or drive a boat by themselves. How old should a kid be before they can go out camping on their own? Should kids even be able to drive? At the root of these discussions is fear. As adults, we make way too many decisions based on fear. And most of the time, we don't even realize it.

Back in 2005, when I was a volunteer firefighter, I hopped on an engine one day and came home thirty-three days later in a wheelchair after getting burned in the grass fire I'd been fighting. Today, one of the most common questions I'm asked is: "Aren't you afraid to be out fighting fires after you got hurt?"

My smart-aleck response always gets a confused look in return: "Nope, I learned that the red part is hot!"

I'm able to handle the question this way because of what I learned about fear growing up, and because of what I was able to test in my life as a wildland firefighter in the years after I was burned.

As kids, we are fearless because we're ignorant. You don't know that skunks are bad until your dad says you can't bring one in the house to show Mom. That spring runoff in the creek is *really* cold when you jump into it playing army in March. Who knew that you're not supposed to shoot fireworks off of a dry hay bale in July?

Yep, all true stories.

It isn't until we start getting hurt—or, more often, until we start watching the reaction of those older than us—that we start learning to be afraid. The older we get, the more we choose to either be afraid of the things we're told to be afraid of or ignore them. The result: We end up with people who are afraid and people who are not. When it comes to life and the outdoors, neither group is a safe one to be a part of.

I would like to inject another word into the discussion. That word is *respect*. It's a word we all know but forget to use and, more importantly, practice.

Now, I'm sure some of you are thinking: What does respect have to do with being afraid or not? The answer is: everything. To respect something means you have to study it and do your best to understand it. You need to learn what it's capable of.

The day I was burned, I was the guy who chose not to be afraid of fire. I was out there battling because most people *are* afraid of fire. The bad thing happened that day because of our lack of respect for the power of fire.

When I started to study fire behavior, I began to understand how and why fire acts the way it does. That was when I learned to *respect* fire. The reason I'm not afraid of fire today is that I respect it. Once I started to respect fire, I

It's our responsibility to
get our kids ready for life
on their own.

was able to start making wise decisions about it. Yep, that's right, wise decisions.

This same idea also holds true as we raise our kids.

It's our responsibility to get our kids ready for life on their own. But when we're afraid of all the things that could go wrong, we put our kids in a position where they need to choose to fear or not to fear. If, on the other hand, we take the time to learn with our kids about the things we're afraid of, we learn how to respect those things together.

*It's important
to let kids discover.*

So instead of scolding a child for playing in the fire, teach them how fire behaves and what's wise to do and what's not wise to do with it. It doesn't matter if it's a vehicle, a boat, summer, winter, river, lake, ice, snowmobile, or gun; we need to teach kids the potential of the things we encounter in life and in the outdoors.

As kids grow, give them opportunities to learn and understand the power of nature and the equipment we use in the outdoors. In 2011, as I noted earlier, we had a chance as a family to help clean up after a major flood in a nearby town. We all got to see firsthand the power that a small, meandering river can have. The lessons we learned there have led to many discussions about the big, slow river we live on now and what Mother Nature is capable of.

It's also important to let kids practice and fail in small, safe ways so that they can build the experience they need to become proficient later in life. I'll never forget our family's first trip to the Boundary Waters Canoe Area in northern Minnesota. Sons Dan and Peter were showing the little kids how to canoe. The four of them were all facing each other and paddling as hard as they could. I wasn't worried about them getting lost, though, because they could only go in circles.

As the kids got older, they helped with the maintenance of the motor on the boat and learned how to drive the boat all by themselves. Learning to respect the boat is just as important as learning to respect the river and the weather. As parents, we get to oversee as our kids learn and as they practice making wise decisions. We can stretch them when we see they're ready to move on to the next experience level.

The result is worth the time you invest. It's amazing how freeing it is to get fear out of your life. As a parent, you're no longer counting on hope to keep your kids safe because you've taught them how to make good decisions. Likewise, our kids know their own capabilities and limitations instead of rebelling against something their parents are afraid of.

When we learn to respect the outdoors and the tools we bring into the outdoors, we all make wise decisions instead of being afraid.

As I said: This requires time. But it's also *a conscious decision*. It's not what we naturally want to do. But it's worth the investment in the long run. Not only does it help us confront fear in a positive way; it also builds and strengthens the relationships in your family.

part four

THE FUTURE

You'll never arrive if you
don't pick where you want to go.

chapter 33

PICKING A DESTINATION

You know that time of year when we plan all the stuff we're going to do for the rest of the year? Events, trips, vacations. All the stuff we didn't do last year.

We all know someone who is calculating out the hunting-lottery applications they need to place in different states so that they can get more preference points they need to get the tag they want in the right year to fit their plan. When I was growing up, my family focused on buying permits for the Boundary Waters Canoe Area in northern Minnesota for the upcoming summer.

What's important in this process is picking a destination. Some destinations take years to get access to, whereas with others you can just up and decide to go. Here's the thing, though: It doesn't matter what it takes to get there; you'll never arrive if you don't pick where you want to go.

For most families, one of the craziest times in raising kids is when you're choosing, budgeting, and planning for vacations like big hunting or fishing trips. This all comes, of course, before the enjoyment and/or stresses of navigating through all the logistical stuff that accompanies a once-a-year trip.

This is the time to take a deep breath and let all the memories that are knocking at the door of your brain flood in. I want you to look them all over, both the happy and the not so happy. Some of you grew up in homes where trips flowed smoothly. Others of you dreaded thinking about a trip because of how ugly the memories were.

One of the principles I learned growing up is that "everything goes according to plan, especially when you don't have one." When it comes to raising kids, this is most certainly true. When it comes to raising kids in anticipation of the biggest, most important trip of your life, having a plan is a major difference between good memories and bad.

Your trip's potential for a good—or bad—outcome starts with picking a destination. How do you know if "we're there yet" if you don't know where you're going? For every trip, every family needs to pick a destination, a mode of travel, a budget, a duration, and activities that fit them vs. someone else. Most people don't realize it until it's too late, but when you're raising kids, you can't copy someone else's travel plans.

I've said several times throughout this book that every kid is different. That idea comes roaring into play in picking a destination, too. Have you ever thought about asking the question: "What's the destination for each of my kids?" My wife and I want to raise kids who are productive members of society and who love God. Along the way, we want to teach them how to be self-reliant and have a solid work ethic, all while putting others' needs before their own. Every kid's journey is different, and as parents it's our responsibility to teach them the skills and principles that will help each of them reach their own unique destination.

What's nice about picking out a destination for your journey is that it helps you make decisions along the way and removes a lot of the stress involved. We all come to forks in the road and construction zones that require us to change direction. When we don't have a destination, we don't know if the new road we choose will get us where we don't know where we're going ... yep, it makes your head hurt!

The trail doesn't matter.
the direction does.

But when we know where we're going, we can easily make decisions. All we have to do is ask: "Does this trail get us to our destination?" If the answer is yes, we can take the trail. The trail doesn't matter, actually; the direction does. If the trail leads away from the destination, don't make a big deal about it; just don't go that way. If you think back on your family trips growing up, the bad memories usually revolve around stress stemming from lack of planning, getting lost, being undecided, and making a big deal out of simple things. On the journey of raising kids, it's no different.

I'll never forget one of the days I asked our boys if they wanted to go fishing. Their answer—in a nutshell, "no"—took me off my feet, partially because I really, really wanted to go fishing but also because I didn't realize we were at a fork in the road.

I looked at the boys and asked a follow-up question: "Why don't you want to go fishing?"

My oldest looked at me and, with all the confidence in the world, replied: "Fishing is boring."

My cartoon bubble was in **bold print**, ALL CAPS:

"HOLD ON, FISHING IS BORING?!"

Fortunately my mouth stayed closed long enough to form a functional, clarifying question: "Why do you think fishing is boring?"

The response was interesting: "We catch too many fish."

I didn't know that was possible, but okay, we catch too many fish.

"What would you rather do on a calm, warm spring day?" I asked in return.

That's when Daniel interjected his thoughts into the conversation: "We want to go shoot."

So I looked at them and said: "Okay, let's go shoot."

It wasn't the road I had picked for the day. But it got us closer to the same destination.

PICKING A DESTINATION

This is just a fun, simple snapshot of our family's journey. Yet most of life's questions become this simple when we know where we're going. Doesn't matter if it's fishing, hunting, sports, art, fill in the blank; it's about learning together along the journey.

And this is true regardless of the road you're picking, whether it involves the day's activities, a school, or a career. When we pick a destination, we know where we're going and when we get there.

I'm a big fan of gifts that create opportunities for kids and parents to use the gift together.

chapter 34

PRESENTS
THAT WORK

When Christmas is just around the corner, most parents are still trying to figure out the perfect gifts for their kids. At the same time, many grandparents are wondering if the grand-kids are going to like the gifts they bought for them five to ten months ago! And we can't forget the aunts, uncles, and friends who are out there buying presents for your kids to get even for something you did to them long ago.

Yep, Christmas is coming. And for many, it's a time of confusion and indecision about what to get kids as gifts.

As I've mentioned before, one of my favorite gifts grow-ing up was a paperback book. As you may have realized by now, it's strange for me to have a favorite *anything* that involves a book. Dyslexic kids don't like books, as a rule. But this book I more than liked.

In the interest of full disclosure: It was also the item that got me into more trouble with my mom than any other gift I have ever received. Ever. *How to Make Your Own Lures and Flies*, by Mel Marshall. I'd like to think that Mel has some level of culpability in all that trouble I got into. I mean, really: If Mom was telling me I needed to read books and then I ended up cutting apart some of her silverware to make pike spoons and walleye jigging spoons like Mel taught in the book I had chosen to read, shouldn't Mom and Mel figure out who I was supposed to listen to? Just sayin'.

On a slightly more serious note: What this gift did for me is unleash my creativity on a constructive activity I loved: fishing. In all reality, it's probably the genesis of Missouri Secrets Tackle, the company my sons own and operate. This book has also helped me arrive at some principles my wife and I use to pick out gifts for our own kids. And yes—I do try to "look" like I avoid gifts that get the kids in trouble with their mom.

The first thing we look for in gifts for our kids is *not* what they want or currently like. Instead, we look ahead to what they're exploring and what they're going to be doing in the upcoming year. Then we get them gifts that allow them to further explore those areas of life or that help them achieve an upcoming milestone. For one of our boys, for example, we picked out a set of reloading dies that matched the rifle he was saving up for. For our daughter, it was sketch pads and all the pencils and charcoal she could handle.

What's important is understanding your kids so that you have a good sense of where they're going and how you can give them the tools, vision, and motivation to become who they are. If they're an artist, angler, athlete, etc., then get them gifts that help them become an artist, angler, athlete, etc.

Next, give gifts with meaning and without strings attached. This is a big deal. When we give gifts with meaning, we build relationships with our kids. Trust me when I say this: If you give a gift to pacify a child, your relationship with that child will suffer. Giving gifts with meaning and without any expectations demonstrates to kids that you care.

I remember the year my dad gave me a check for a hundred dollars for Christmas—with a note saying he wished he could give me that much but that the money wasn't in the bank. Without thinking about it, I tore the check in half, looked at him, and said: "It's okay." And then, with a hug, he gave me a box to open. Inside was a small LEGO set from grade school, with a note directing me to head outside to the shed.

Give gifts that unleash your kids' creativity.

There, I found my first ice house—which Dad had worked to get for me. I can't explain what that gift meant to me, because I knew what it had taken to make it possible.

I'm not a big fan of giving gifts that kids deserve. There are things in life that kids have earned, and it works out best in the end if you give kids the thing they've earned as a reward for earning it. I know this is kind of vague, but the things I'm talking about are different for every kid. Most of our kids have, over the years, received a rod and reel as a gift. But as the older boys started to work for me, we made it a point to give them the gear they earned not *as gifts*, but *for their work*.

The first lead pot and mold was a gift. Now, jig molds are part of the business.

For example, having a kid earn their first firearm is important and brings with it many valuable lessons that they wouldn't get if the firearm were to be given to them as a gift. But as kids get older, giving them a firearm they can't afford as a gift for a milestone in life builds upon the lessons they learned when they earned their first firearm. There's something to defining a gift as something the person doesn't deserve but is given simply because someone cared.

Like I said, it's vague. Because to get it right, you have to understand your kid. And every kid is different.

I *am* a big fan of gifts that create opportunities for kids and parents to use the gift together. Raising kids is all about building relationships. Spending time together is one of the key ingredients. Several years ago, Grandma and Grandpa got the kids an ice saw, a spear, and some fish decoys. We have had so much fun as a family failing to spear a pike. It was a gift with a built-in challenge and exploration, not to mention some physical activity that I am more than willing to watch the kids undertake. Gifts you get to share together provide a lot of fun and lifelong stories.

Finally, don't worry about picking out the "right" or "wrong" gifts. Just spend some time learning about the kids in your life and find gifts that help teach them who they are and build relationships. In the end, it's not about how much money you spend; it's about how much you care.

And if you're lucky, Mom won't even miss the spoons from the drawer after the gifts are opened.

We worry if they're ready,
but the question is: Are we ready?

chapter 35

ARE THEY READY?

One of the hardest things for me to watch when it comes to outdoor experiences is a dad and his kid at the store, hurriedly picking out a first bow or gun during the opening week of hunting season. Witnessing this scene is difficult not only because the kid is getting set up for failure, but also because there are lifelong ramifications that follow.

To avoid those ramifications, all we as adults need to do is think ahead, spend time understanding the kids we're heading out with in the fall, and have lots of fun with them getting ready for the upcoming season.

I am writing this, by the way, in full disclosure of both my successes and failures as a parent in the outdoors. I'll cover what I've learned from what works *and* what hasn't.

First step: You need to know and understand each kid's abilities, limitations, and, most importantly, desires. This is true whether you're picking out a fishing rod, a gun, a bow, or what game to hunt. With the ever-growing number of youth opportunities that are out there, we as adults need to be observant enough to know whether each kid is physically and mentally ready for each of those opportunities.

Picking the right equipment is huge, but it doesn't have to break the bank.

For example: All four of our kids took advantage of North Dakota's youth doe season each September, but none of them used the same gun; they were all different sizes and had different shooting abilities.

I still feel guilty about how I screwed this one up when it came to son Peter's first year of archery hunting. The year before, we had set the standard of a five-inch group at twenty-five yards, from all angles and positions. Peter is the kid who has a burning desire to be in the outdoors, and he shot every morning and night to be good enough to meet the standard so that he could go deer hunting with a stick and string.

But like most kids, Peter had a growth spurt. So three weeks before the season, we had to get him a new bow because he had outgrown his other one. He continued to shoot well, though, so we hit the tree stand.

On our first night there, a doe walked in at seventeen yards. Peter slowly stood up, aimed, and let the arrow fly. But to my surprise, he only grazed the front of the deer, and we were both frustrated.

For the next two weeks, I worked with him on all the mental things he'd done wrong that had caused him to miss the deer. But he continued getting frustrated because he had lost all consistency while he was practicing. Until one day, he asked the question I still feel guilty about:

"Dad, why is my sight moving?"

Yep. All our troubles had been the result of the sight coming loose on Peter's new bow.

This is where I had screwed up. I knew Peter's capabilities and limitations, yet I had trusted the bow shop more. A shop I'd had only a handful of experiences with. Once we tightened up the bow sight, Peter was back to his old shooting form. And that night, we went back to the tree stand and he got his first deer with a bow.

To be ready for the outdoors, I now have a handful of principles I follow to keep incidents like this one from happening again.

GOALS, NOT DATES

First, set goals, not dates. This approach takes a lot of the pressure off of both you and the kid. Neither of you has any control over how the kid grows and matures physically, which naturally affects both hand-eye coordination and muscle memory.

One of the worst times in life for kids—a time we as adults tend to forget, even though we probably lived through it ourselves—is when they are growing so fast that their coordination goes out the window. They're big enough to handle a lot, but if they jumped at the ground at that point, they would miss.

Set individual goals, and let each kid get to them at their own pace. Never compare kids to other kids. When they meet each goal, celebrate—and then set new ones.

EQUIPMENT THAT FITS

Picking the right equipment is huge. I can't tell you how many people I know who don't shoot or hunt today because they had a bad experience with a gun that was too big or, more importantly, too lightweight for them. Throw in stories about bad boots or the wrong clothes for the trip and you can sum up most horror stories that stick with kids.

No, I'm not made of money. I do, however, love garage sales, hand-me-downs, and friends. Make sure you have the right equipment for the excursion and the kid. It makes a difference.

SHORT PRACTICES

Over the years, I have found that more, short practices are better than fewer, marathon practices. During the summer, we will go to the range multiple times and shoot five rounds each with the deer rifles we'll be using that fall. On some trips to the range, we will pick a single position to work on. During other trips, we will take five shots from five different positions, all while encouraging each other (although I should say that apparently, there

Just because you're hunting doesn't mean you can't answer questions.

is room for mocking Dad when he shoots worse than Mom; I have been so informed by the kids). Similarly, shooting two to five arrows each morning or evening is more effective than a fifteen- to thirty-minute shoot.

When it comes to shooting clay pigeons, make sure to quit before the kids' arms start getting tired or sore. The reason: muscle memory. Even as adults, when our muscles get fatigued, we compensate and start practicing with bad stance, bad hand position, etc.—which, of course, ingrains bad habits and bad technique.

The other perk to the "short practices" principle is that you have many more opportunities to see growth and meet goals.

LEARNING AND
REALISTIC EXPECTATIONS

This principle is important both for the outdoor experience and for parenting in general. We need to give kids *learning experiences* in the outdoors, not set unrealistic expectations for and of them.

Whether you want to believe it or not, life and the outdoors aren't fair. If we set expectations based on numbers, kills, and time of kills, we set our kids up for failure. Instead, we need to focus on teaching, learning together, and being satisfied with what nature provides.

Never put a kid in a position where they think it's their fault, and never make them feel guilty for not filling a tag or not getting a limit on a particular day. It's more important to learn the whys than to fall into the trap of blame.

START EARLY

Finally, start early. "As soon as you can see the range through the melted snow" is a good time to start practicing and getting ready. But when I say "start early," I'm also speaking more broadly to those of you who have kids who will be starting out one or two years from now.

Spend time learning together the weapon each kid will be using in the fall, the game you'll be pursuing, and the locations you'll be hunting. It's a lot of fun because you get to hike together, talk together, and shoot together. Starting early has more impact on whether you will fill a tag or get a limit than does setting expectations or hopes.

The definition of success in the outdoors—as we've discussed all along here—is having a positive experience. Sometimes the positive experience is fun, sometimes it's hard. The key is that we and our kids are ready to learn together so that we have that positive experience in the outdoors no matter what happens.

Being ready is worth it, and you will be surprised how much you learn about the outdoors and your kids when you are *getting* ready together.

Don't forget to have a *camera* ready, too, so that you can document whatever happens. That way, you can share the stories about what you've learned and experienced for years to come.

Having a plan prevents heartache come hunting season.

chapter 36

PLANNING AHEAD

One of the keys to having fun in the outdoors is having a plan.

Now, before you say it: My wife and I have four kids. All of them are involved in sports and all sorts of other extra-curricular activities. The answer is "yes": Having a plan *does* seem like an unachievable dream. That's why I'm writing about having a plan. It is not only achievable; it's vital if you want to have successful outdoor experiences with your kids over the coming years.

Let's get this thing started on the right foot: When I'm talking about planning ahead, I'm talking about a loose set of goals that includes the activities you'd like to do with your family over the next two to three years. For new parents, this may seem like a long time out. But trust me: Time really does go really fast.

Your plan needs to be a flexible guideline that makes sense for your kids as they develop their outdoor skills and ambitions. Always make sure you meet your kids where they are.

Next, use the plan to set priorities—so that you can keep your kids from the disappointments that almost always lead back to lack of planning on our part as adults.

Every fall, I meet parents who talk about how excited they are to take their kids hunting for the first time that year. They've been out shooting, scouting, and shopping with their kids to get ready for the upcoming season. It's always tough when they ask me—right before the season starts—where and when they can take a hunter safety class. In many places, these classes are offered in the *spring*, because most instructors are hunting during the fall. In many cases, then, this ends the dreams parents and kids have of a first hunting season together.

The same thing happens when parents set an age that their kids are going to get their first deer. This past fall, for instance, I talked to a dad who had done everything necessary to get his kid ready for youth deer season. But then he talked to his wife about the school activities his son was committed to ... yep, no deer hunting this year.

That's why planning ahead helps.

One year, our family had our last kid taking driver's education class. It took place during the first two weeks of June. We had worked with the school and changed our obligations for the big charity fishing tournament we help with during that time so that we could make everything work. It was only possible because we were planning ahead, and so we had talked as a family to make priorities we all agreed on.

That same year, our sons Peter and Andrew were fishing the Student Angler Tournament Trail in Minnesota again. One of them was also going to play baseball, and both had jobs to boot. The only way it all worked was with a simple plan that was communicated to and agreed upon by everyone.

*Make sure to compare
all the calendars.*

Here's where to start on the planning process. Take a good look at the skill levels of your kids. Then, mix in their likes and dislikes for the outdoors with the must-haves for the activities they want to participate in. There's a reason I talked earlier about having a *loose* plan, one that is two to three years ahead: You don't want to be caught off guard when kids change their mind, have a growth spurt, or mature sooner than you expected. So look for a hunter safety class a year before your child needs it. Look into the archery options that would best fit your child before they're ready to start. Planning ahead helps things go more smoothly and allows everyone to be ready for the season *before* it starts.

When you've made priorities as a family, you can take advantage of opportunities when they come along.

Be sure to factor in school and activity calendars and compare them with the outdoor activities you have in mind. As a family, make some decisions based on who your kids are and what will benefit them the most. Remember: This is different for every kid. Some kids need the break from school, others need the one-on-one time with a parent, and still others need the extra time to get homework done. What's important is that *you* make decisions that make sense for each kid. Don't be swayed by what *other* people think. Besides: If you try to force a kid to like something, or you try to keep them from doing something they're good at, things will end badly. Guaranteed.

PLANNING AHEAD

Over the last ten-plus years, I have been on call to leave home in short order to help with wildfires somewhere in the United States. Having a plan like the one I'm talking about here has been the glue that has kept our outdoor activities doable, and has ensured that everyone is ready when the time comes to get outside.

As parents, it's easy to get caught up in working to give our kids a good life and being able to afford to get them into the outdoors. So take some reflective time to understand your kids, figure out the direction they're going, mark up a calendar, avoid the letdowns, and enjoy the outdoors together.

It's okay to skip out on some things
to enjoy other activities.

chapter 37

JUGGLING

Oh, the weather outside is frightful, but the fire is so delightful, and since we've no place to go ... well, that's not the case!

I have three Christmas concerts to go to, plus a basketball tournament, family parties in two cities, a turkey tag, early ice, two youth archery tags, late goose season, and a whole lot more that my wife told me about but I can't remember.

If you have kids, you know I am dramatically *understating* the reality of fall hunting, fishing, school, family, and holiday season. In other words, parenting life.

Well, if you're at the beginning of this crazy season, you're most likely thinking it will never end and never get any better. Many people, on the other hand, long to get these days back. And some of us are coming out the tail end of the season with endless stories to tell. Sure, some of them are bad. But most are good and, in hindsight, worth it all. Meantime, sitting outside the arena is the group of folks who aren't here yet or never will be—making statements that start with "when I have kids..." and "you should..."

Regardless of the season of life *you* are in, grab a cup of coffee and follow along. I have a to-do list for everyone. Yep, everyone.

BYSTANDERS

First, a quick word to those of you who are on the outside looking in on the juggling act called parenting. When you're watching from afar, it's really easy to come up with a list of how you could do things easier, smarter, better.

Well, don't take this wrong but ... zip it.

Don't say a word. Here are a few things you need to understand.

Unlike popular opinions, every kid and situation is different. And only the people connected to each other know all the variables involved. Your job is to be a cheerleader, not a coach or an inspector. Let parents know they have a hard job, and that you respect them for it.

PARENTS

If you're a parent yourself, memorize these two truths:

It's worth it.

You will make it.

(Dads, we need to remind our wives about these truths often, not just when they're overwhelmed ... because that doesn't work. Maybe I can cover how I know that in a future first-aid book.)

Here's what we as parents need to remember: We need to raise each of our kids to be who *they* are, not what we want them to be—and definitely not what someone else wants them to be.

When it comes to juggling all the family, school, outdoors, sports, and other activities, here are a few things to consider and remember.

You and your kids don't need to do it all. So sit down with them and establish some priorities. As parents, we have the insight and, more importantly, the heart to understand our kids. You know better than anyone if your kid needs to be in school that day or in the blind instead. You know what it takes to motivate them and stretch them. You know what lessons they need to learn and whether they're best learned on the court, in the field, on the ice, in the studio, in the pew, or in the classroom. Pick the activities that fit each kid best and know that it's okay not to do other activities.

The relationship-building that happens when you pick the schedules you're going to juggle is worth every minute.

Youth deer seasons are a great example. You have any-where from three to ten days to get a young hunter into the field to get their first deer. But if you have a kid who's involved in sports, you suddenly have two or three sched-ules to juggle.

For some of our own kids, we found a spot close to home that we could get to in ten minutes, then sat there for an hour and a half after football practice. One year, my daughter chose to get a muley buck youth tag, so we skipped some school and volleyball practices to spend a couple of long weekends hunting in the badlands. At the end of the day, the relationship-building that hap-pens when we pick the schedules we're going to juggle is worth every minute.

You have only one shot at raising your kids, and you're the only parents they will ever have. Nothing is more important to your kids than their relationship with you. We will always have work to do, rooms to clean, stuff to learn. But we only have a limited time when our kids say things like "Can we go duck hunting in the morning?" when they know full well it's only going to be six degrees outside. As crazy as it seems at times, make sure you always take advantage of the one thing only you can do: be a parent to your kids. Yes, even at six degrees.

You won't always get it right. You'll sometimes be upset because you'll give up things you want to do. That's normal. But it's worth it. Love your kids. Love the time you spend with them. Apologize when it's obvious that you've done something wrong and, more importantly, apologize when no one knows you got it wrong.

The whole point of learning to juggle is to build relationships with your kids, whether you're in the outdoors or at a baseball game.

GRANDPARENTS

Grandparents: You've been there, and you know how hard the juggling act is for parents. So take the opportunity to be a *spotter*: Catch, without judgment, the things that get dropped.

You have the unique privilege of bringing clarity to life for your kids and grandkids. Don't try to do the things your body has put on the "not to do" list. But do what you *can* do when the need arises.

Remember: Your words have power. Use that power to help build relationships. Whether it's in the boat, in the blind, in the kitchen, in the shop, or around the campfire, take the time to share your insights and to bring your history to life.

OUTDOOR ENTHUSIASTS

I've already talked about all the things I learned from my dad, but he couldn't catch a fish to save his life. He never hunted, either. So he didn't know what to teach me about either activity.

Thankfully, there was a group of guys who took time to take me out fishing, shooting clay pigeons, and hunting for my first deer. These men helped out in the areas my dad couldn't. They didn't replace him. They simply reinforced him in their roles as mentors to me.

Today, there are lots of families whose kids (and perhaps adults, too!) would love to take part in outdoor activities. They just need mentors. If you're an outdoor enthusiast, it's your job to help where you can. Meet people where they are. You can either take the kids out to teach them what you know, or you can go out with the parents to teach *them* outdoor skills—so that they in turn can teach their kids themselves.

Let's be honest: It isn't that hard to have to go hunting or fishing in the name of helping someone else, is it?

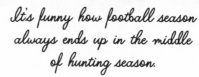

It's funny how football season always ends up in the middle of hunting season.

ADMINISTRATORS

Whether you're a leader at school, church, work, or elsewhere, know this: Families that participate in the outdoors together are families that live life together. And families that live life together are families that are easier to work with.

My sons Dan and Peter always knew that if they kept their grades up, they could ask to get out of school or church to hit the water when the bite was on. I loved watching them run to the truck midafternoon so that we could get in the night bite during early ice. I can testify in a court of law that in grade school, the boys had higher grades because they knew they'd get more time with Mom and Dad in the outdoors—way more than they would have gotten had our family followed a rigid schedule.

If you're an administrator, you can help parents juggle schedules for a positive outcome. Or you can be the one who knocks all the balls to the ground. Please do your part and meet parents and kids where they are.

As I write this, my wife and I are juggling more than I think we can handle—just like every other parent. We know, though, that it's possible because we can always count on help, particularly from the mentors in our family's life.

What I know for sure is that learning life together as a family, in the outdoors and elsewhere, is worth every minute. And juggling is one of the key skills that makes it possible.

All I have to say is: It's bigger than my brother's deer.

chapter 38

PRIORITIES

I've had a lot of fun over the years writing about the principles we use in our family to raise our kids in the outdoors. But as I've shared our journey and all the fun stories from along the way, a misconception has emerged among some readers:

"Man, you guys are always out hunting and fishing."

I wish this were true, but it's not.

Like every other family, we have decisions to make. And a lot of the time, those decisions aren't so easy. So I thought I'd share with you how we as a family use *priorities* to make our decisions throughout the year, and how those decisions change kid to kid and year to year.

Let me start out with one of my mistakes from this past year.

It was youth deer season in September, and my daughter Morgan and I were sitting in the blind, waiting for some does to come out on the second day. Sure enough, right before sunset, a group of deer came out. They were lazily eating their way through the cut alfalfa field and had no clue we were there. The nicest doe was 167 yards out and was an easy shot for Morgan. So we repositioned in the blind, and she took aim and shot.

As I watched in the binoculars, I saw that it had not been a clean shot. So I told Morgan: "Rack another one." She did and dropped the deer at a dead run.

As I gave her a hug and we were celebrating her getting her second deer, I was thinking to myself: *"Why didn't she get a clean shot the first time?"* As we were leaving the blind, she handed me the gun and I realized what I had done wrong: I hadn't changed my priorities with Morgan at the gun range from those I'd had for her the year before. I had also forgotten what I'd taught to whom that year. More specifically in this instance: I hadn't worked with Morgan on how to choose the correct power on her scope for the distance she was shooting by herself.

Why do priorities matter so much where kids and parents are concerned? There's a long list of answers to that question, but here are the reasons my wife and I see as most important when it comes to the outdoors.

I suspect that for most of you reading this book, the outdoors is a way of life. But too often, when it comes to kids and families, people get their priorities all messed up, and the family suffers for it. When I say that, I'm not pointing at any specific activity(ies). What I'm saying is that some people have priorities that hurt the other people in their lives. These are the priorities that are wrong. As a family, it's important to set priorities that build up those we love and care about.

Life is full of opportunities, and many parents and grandparents break their backs to get their kids into (and to!) as many of these opportunities as possible. But there's nothing wrong with picking just one or two things to do each year.

As a family, talk about the potential opportunities and then set some priorities for the upcoming year. That way, everyone is on the same page—so that when conflicts inevitably come up, the decisions are easier. This makes life way easier when it comes to the outdoors, sports, and kids. There are no wrong answers. Just make sure everyone, including teachers and coaches, is in general agreement. For the last few years, for example, our son Andrew has been playing baseball. So we are always in the process of talking over his commitments and setting priorities where summer is concerned.

As parents, we have goals and aspirations for our kids. What many of us parents tend to forget, though, is to ask our kids what *their* dreams and aspirations are. As the Proverb says: It's our job to raise up our kids the way they are to be. I've said it before: If we have an athlete, we need to raise an athlete. If we have an artist, we need to raise an artist. If we have an engineer, we need to raise an engineer. It's important to prioritize so that your kids can achieve *their* dreams and aspirations.

And yes: Their dreams and aspirations can, and often do, change a lot. That's normal. Part of being a kid is exploring and learning.

Long before our son Peter figured out how much he liked fishing, he was focused on being the best muskrat trapper in the state. He bought some traps and read all the books he could find so we could trap muskrats in the winter.

Peter's first year of trapping went okay, and he made some money and bought some more traps. Year two, however, was a different story. That year, there was less water and fewer rats. That meant that Peter's mornings got earlier, and his walks longer, all for little return. That year, Peter's priorities changed—and so did ours as his parents.

It's okay that priorities change as kids grow up.

One misconception I hear a lot is that it takes money to set priorities. But I would argue that the most critical and valuable currency when it comes to priorities is *time*. There are lots of things that our family just can't afford to buy. Learning to duck hunt, for example, was on our family's list a couple of years ago. We simply asked around and found some folks to take us out. Once we learned what we needed, we spent time together as a family building blinds so that we could go hunting together. One of our priorities is spending time together. Time costs nothing. The kids, however, did have to do some side jobs to cover all the steel shot.

Please understand: Setting priorities is not an exact science, and my wife and I make plenty of mistakes in parenting. It's important that our kids know this, and that we as parents share it with them in a gracious, loving way. This is a life changer when they grow up. If you raise kids *hoping* they grow up okay, they don't. When you raise kids intentionally, on the other hand, you understand who they are, and you can better mold them into who they were created to be. Setting priorities together as a family is an essential part of raising kids intentionally. It takes the hope out of parenting and replaces it with confidence, at home and in the field.

Let me repeat something I've said previously in this book: We only get to be the parents to our kids once. Prioritize the time to be with them so that you can intentionally invest in them. Whether it's the outdoors, a play, church, a robotics contest, needed time alone, or (gasp!) even baseball: You will never regret setting priorities. And your kids will thank you for it.

It's important to take part in activities with your kids that you are just as proficient at as they are.

chapter 39

SUMMER PROJECTS, DUCKS, AND KIDS

The pandemic summer of 2020 was vastly different than previous summers. Depending on what state you live in, you experienced a variety of limitations due to the COVID-19 situation.

Yes, it would be easy to be upset and frustrated about all the things you and your family missed. That summer, my business wasn't allowed to operate, sports were canceled for our kids, and there was no clear direction on how long things would be that way.

I'd like to throw out a different way of looking at this strange time in our lives: What about all the things we suddenly had time for?

As I look back on my life growing up, the most memorable and influential times revolved around two things: summer projects and lack of money. One summer when I was in high school, for example, Dad decided we needed a canoe trailer so that we could take more people canoeing. As we looked around at trailers, it was evident that we couldn't afford to buy one. So we started pricing out materials and scrounged around for the parts we'd need to build our own trailer. When all was said and done, we pulled it off for a couple hundred dollars. And after a few shakedown trips, we made it to the Boundary Waters Canoe Area in northern Minnesota (and back!) with our summer project.

I always loved summer projects because I got to spend time with my dad. Now, one or two years later, I love working on summer projects with my own kids.

You don't need to spend a lot of money on summer projects.

This is the same reason I love duck hunting with my kids: I get to spend time with them in the blind. Sure, I stink at duck hunting—as in no-hope-of-ever-being-successful-at water-fowling stink. My record for a thirty-five-year stretch is one goose and maybe a dozen ducks. Fortunately, though, that's not what it's about when we're talking about kids. It's about time and learning together.

SUMMER PROJECTS, DUCKS, AND KIDS

During COVID summer 2020, my daughter Morgan, youngest son Andrew, and I went to the local lumberyard and picked up some cheap PVC pipe and a couple of cans of spray paint, to go with some used burlap we had rummaged up. When we got home, we took the pipe and started putting it together in different ways until a plan came together. After a couple of nights trying many different configurations, we arrived on a collapsible blind for duck season. There are better blinds at the store, but this blind is priceless. We are already making many family memories in it.

We're now in the process of turning our old boat and a couple of canoes into duck boats. We always keep an eye out for sales to buy the supplies for projects when they come up. We've spent time in some old books, too, learning how to paint proper camouflage to hide from those pesky ducks. And we're working together to paint and repaint until (we think) we're ready for duck season.

Now, you might be wondering: "What's up with all the duck hunting projects if you're a failure of a duck hunter?" Good question. It's important to take part in activities with your kids that you are just as proficient at as they are. It's also important to provide an environment for you and your kids to be free to talk, without distractions and, most critically, without judgment. I've been (re)learning this lesson ever since the first duck hunting trip I took with my kids.

In all the years since that first outing, the kids have asked me a lot of questions about a lot of things. Some questions are easy, some harder to answer. That's why I can't wait to get into the blind with the kids each fall. With all the stuff happening in the world, there will be a lot of deep, thoughtful discussions in between ducks coming in.

If you've been paying attention, you know by now a couple of key things about me. First, my definition of success is having a positive outdoor experience. And second, I believe strongly in spending time learning together because of how it builds solid relationships with your kids. What you may not know about me is that I don't like getting skunked any more than the next guy. So, on the duck hunting front, I've done what many people are afraid to do ...

I've asked for help. Yep, help.

If we're honest about it, help is a lesson we all hate to learn. It's in our nature to have the "I can do it myself" attitude. But duck hunting is one of several activities in my life that has taught me that I do need to ask for help sometimes. Everyone does.

Over a period of several years, I asked a lot of people for help with duck hunting. I got no response, but I kept asking. Finally one summer, a group of guys from Ducks Unlimited said they'd love to help—and help they did. They took us out on a handful of mentored hunts, where we learned what we'd been doing wrong in the past and what it would take to be successful in the future. We learned about picking the right water, what shells to use, and how to update our homemade blind, all so we could have a better chance of bringing home some ducks.

The real question here, the bigger life question, is: How are you going to handle adversity, especially in a COVID type of situation? Will you shut down your life because of what's happening in the world, or will you instead take the opportunity to create with your kids so that you can all get outdoors and spend time together?

As parents, we don't know it all. So it's okay to ask for help when we need it. And regardless of the circumstances we face at any given time, we can *spend* time with our kids. It's valuable time because we're all learning together.

Even though the COVID years have been difficult, I get to be optimistic—in part thanks to the lessons I've learned preparing for and then going duck hunting with my kids. That's why I love summer projects, ducks, and kids.

I love summer projects, ducks, and kids.

It's always about meeting kids where they are
and having a positive outdoor experience.

OUTDOOR SPORTS

Growing up, I never dreamed that kids would one day be able to *compete* in outdoor activities like fishing and shooting. Did you know that the fastest-growing high school sports in the United States right now are angling, archery, and trap shooting? There are lots of reasons for this growth, and even more questions parents have about what it takes to get involved.

So my wife and I sat down and talked about all the concerns, frustrations, and blessings we've encountered as a family that participates in outdoor sports competitions. We've compiled it all into a few thoughts for parents, coaches, and volunteers to consider when they're exploring involvement in any of the outdoor sports.

IT'S NOT AS HARD AS IT LOOKS

If you've ever had a child in a school-sanctioned activity, you know there are hoops to jump through. Not all of these hoops are complicated or difficult; they're just there.

One of the mistakes Kirsten and I made as our boys were looking into competitive high school fishing was that we

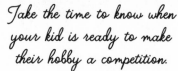

Take the time to know when your kid is ready to make their hobby a competition.

thought we had to jump through the same hoops we jumped through for other high school sports. But that couldn't be further from the truth. Many of the high school sports use the same terminology as your local school sports, but that's where the similarities end. Most outdoor high school activities simply require you to sign up and show up.

So before you write off an outdoor sport as being too much work to be involved in, ask around and see what it *actually* takes to be involved.

IS IT A REAL SPORT?

I've heard a lot of people say that outdoor sports aren't real sports. I strongly disagree.

The purpose of high school sports is to teach students how to win and lose, prepare themselves for success, overcome adversity, stretch themselves, interact with others, and more. It doesn't matter if they're on the football field or walking a 3-D range, kids learn a whole host of life skills through competing in any setting.

The difference between traditional high school sports and outdoor sports is that outdoor sports are available to a wider group of students. You don't have to be in the "top 5 percent of athletes" in your school to compete in outdoor sports. There's an opportunity for almost everyone at any ability level. Not to mention the fact that a lot of scholarship money is given out each year in outdoor sports that is not available in traditional school sports.

HOBBY TO COMPETITION

As I've noted before, one of the most critical things to understand when you're raising kids is that you need to meet them where they are. Encouraging them to participate in outdoor sports is a great way to do this. There are virtually limitless opportunities for kids and parents to get involved in these outdoor sports at the hobby level. And as they grow in their ability, it's a natural progression for them to move into a competitive option.

As a parent (or coach), it's essential to understand where a kid is and not push them in a direction they're not ready for. You don't want to start a kid out competing if they're not ready, and you don't want to keep a kid from competing when they are ready. Remember: It's always about meeting kids where they are and having a positive outdoor experience.

Another great thing about many outdoor sports: There are opportunities for parents and kids to compete together. The beauty of outdoor sports is that it can be both: hobby and competition.

KNOW WHEN TO BE A PARENT AND WHEN TO BE A COACH

Outdoor sports offer great opportunities to compete together as a family. Many of the coaches and boat captains across the country are parents of the athletes. It's important to understand, however, when to be a coach and when to be a parent.

One summer, we got to pre-fish a championship tournament together as a family, and the boys came in with a zero weight on one of the tournament days. In that moment, it was more important to offer them a hug and to tell them how proud we were of how hard they'd competed than it was to break down the technical reasons for their not scoring any fish. After the tournament, we did sit down and talk with them about what had gone right and what had gone wrong—in preparation for future tournaments.

Take the time to understand your kids and decide if it's better to have someone else be their coach or captain—because no one else can be their parent.

LEARNING LIFE LESSONS

As you explore all the ways kids can compete today, don't overlook the many life lessons they can learn.

What's missing from outdoor sports, for example, is a school administration that takes care of all the details. In turn, however, there are fewer limitations on where and when the kids

*Outdoor sports provide
lifelong skills.*

can compete. So sit down with the kids and allow *them* to pick the competitions that are best for them, whether they're local, regional, or national. You can then mentor them through the planning, budgeting, traveling, and practicing required to make the experiences successful.

Help the kids make wise decisions, but don't prevent them from making mistakes. The key to success is failure and learning how not to repeat those failures. There's nothing wrong with not going to a competition when the students haven't done their part to make it possible.

Once again: You need to meet kids where they are. If you give them an opportunity they didn't earn, you only hurt them in the long run.

Outdoor sports allow gifted individuals to excel at the highest levels with limited barriers.

DON'T BREAK THE BANK

You don't have to have all the cool stuff you see on TV to compete in high school outdoor sports. Teaching the fundamentals of the activity your student is competing in is more important than the equipment they have.

It's more valuable, for example, for a shooter to understand the sight picture necessary for their discipline than to have a fancy gun. It's more valuable for an angler to understand how the action and power of a fishing rod affects lure action and hook set than it is to have the nicest rod. It's more valuable for an archer to understand anchor points and consistency than it is to have the nicest arrows on the market. As students become more proficient in their sport, you can *then* purchase items that remove barriers to their advancement.

There's another reason you should be careful about over-doing it on the expensive equipment front. It has to do with how students and coaches are treated on the water and on the range. I can't tell you how many times I've seen a new coach, parent, or student competing and making mistakes that any newcomer would make—only to be treated badly by those around them because of the new equipment they're using and the professional jerseys they're wearing. The public treats competitors based on what they see, not on what they know or understand about the skill level of those competing or coaching. That's why it's essential to start simple and grow with your and your kids' ability levels.

Take the time to dig for the opportunities, both locally and around the country, that best fit your student. At first, Kirsten and I were frustrated that there weren't more opportunities in our area. But after a bit of digging, we discovered that there were multiple competitions within thirty minutes of where we live.

It's all about learning together and growing at your student's pace. So don't be afraid to get involved in outdoor sports. The lessons you'll learn with your kids will be life-long—and memorable.

One simple question can change everything.

chapter 41

DAY ON THE WATER CHALLENGE

As I write this in the middle of the COVID-19 pandemic, people are looking around trying to figure out what to do. Fishing license sales and boat registrations are way up as people are fleeing to the outdoors in an attempt to escape all that is going on in the world. Listen to the news and there are multiple stories about the mental health issues plaguing our country through all the pandemic fallout. Our community, in fact, is right now mourning the loss of a young student to suicide.

I think it's fair to say that you don't have to go far to find a large group of people asking: "What do we do? What *can* we do?"

It's okay to say we aren't prepared for this.

I've been asking the same questions as everyone else over the years. I've spent countless hours on the phone, over coffee, in the blind, and on the water listening to family, friends, and people I've never met before who are asking these same questions.

Over Christmas, as I was having one of these conversations on the ice with my kids, it dawned on me: What is

*There's something calming about
spending time on the water.*

the one thing that has helped me all through life when I've been struggling with what to do? After I was injured as a volunteer firefighter, what was the turning point in my emotional recovery? When I was in high school, what was the event that consistently changed my perspective on life and my direction?

A fishing trip.

Not just any fishing trip. A fishing trip with a question.

As the kids and I sat on the ice that Christmas, talking about all that was going on in their lives, we naturally asked a simple question of each other that we ask our kids (and everyone else) all the time. In fact, until that day, I had never realized how important this little question really is.

"How are you doing?"

It's commonly accepted that kids will never talk to their parents. I would argue that this misconception has nothing to do with the kids and everything to do with the parents believing it. It's simple: Parents who ask "how are you doing?" and then listen without condemning have kids who talk to them—nonstop.

Understand: This outreach activity needs to be an ingrained part of your daily life with kids. And you *earn* the response from them by choosing to love them and listen to them instead of judging and condemning them. Love is a gift; it's free. Respect and trust are earned. Taking the time to listen to your kids demonstrates this concept to them.

When the kids and I asked each other "how are you doing?" on the ice, the answers were very interesting. They covered every aspect of life: *Will there be a high school baseball season? I'm having relationship struggles. What color should I paint my room? Can you lip a minnow?* The discussions were free of fear and filled with interaction. It's no surprise to my wife and me that many of the deepest conversations with our kids happen either on the water or to or from the water.

There's something freeing about spending time with people on the water. It's as if all the assumed expectations are gone and we instinctively know that it's okay to be honest. After I got hurt in the fire in 2005, I had all these unrealistic expectations of what I was supposed to do to take care of my family. I held them all inside because I never felt free to share them with anyone.

Until a local fishing guide called me up and asked me to hit the water with him for the day.

As we fished together that sunny afternoon, he asked the same question we all so routinely, almost automatically ask each other: "How are you doing?" But he asked it in such a way that I knew he truly cared and wanted to know. He didn't need to have any solutions to my problems—and he didn't. He only needed to listen—and he did. That day on the water changed my life for the better because it gave me perspective. It was the day I released into the open all the doubts and shame I felt from getting hurt and letting my family down.

When it boils down to it, most of us want to help people in need but don't know how. It's easy to fix something or throw money at it and hope it gets better. But the great need out there right now—at any time, really—is this: People need a friend to talk to, just like I did the day the guide took me out on the water. They need someone who is willing and able to *listen*. You don't have to have the answers to meet this need. You just have to be available.

Here's what dawned on me on the ice at Christmas; here's the Day on the Water Challenge: Ask someone you know to spend a day on the water with you fishing, hunting, boating, canoeing, kayaking, etc. Then, once you're there, simply ask them: "How are you doing?"

Yep, that's it. Do what you love—with someone else. Start the conversation and take the time to care. If you're not sure where to start, look at home. Take your kids, spouse, brother, sister, mom, or dad. From there, look for someone at work, church, or school to take out on the water.

Again: Don't worry about having the answers to the questions someone might have. You'll find that when you take someone out on the water, life seems to work itself out—simply because you took the time to care. It's not about having the answers; it's about the fact that we all need someone we can work life out with. Together.

Will you take the Day on the Water Challenge?

Perspective, perspective, perspective.

chapter

42

CAMPFIRES, KIDS, AND THE OUTDOORS

My favorite time of the year is looking forward to what I get to do next with my kids in the outdoors. I love walking out the back door and sipping my morning coffee as the kids practice shooting their bows before school. I love all the little things that get me excited for what awaits in the coming weeks before the snow flies.

I can sum it all up into the three core activities that define this time of year for me: hunting, fishing, and campfires. On a good day, all three activities happen in the same twenty-four hours.

This time of year is especially meaningful to me as a parent. I look forward to seeing how it strengthens my relationships with my kids as much as, or more than, experiencing the excitement of what we bag or catch each day. When you're enjoying the outdoors with your kids, they're free of the day-to-day distractions that typically get in the way. On an early, foggy morning in the blind or on a starlit night around the campfire, we as parents get the opportunity to listen to our kids and, better yet, learn who they are.

Knowing and understanding your kids is the most crucial part of parenting. And what better place to *get* to know and understand them than in the outdoors with no distractions.

Whether you're in the boat, onshore, or in a duck or deer blind, sitting with your kids one on one in a beautiful, peaceful environment sparks some pretty funny, and sometimes deeply profound, conversations that rarely happen in any other setting. Not to mention the fact that I have learned more about hunting, fishing, and life by digging into questions the kids have asked that I have never thought of asking myself. There's something about the simplicity mixed with the power of the outdoors that puts life in perspective, for kids and adults alike.

A couple of years ago, my son Andrew and I were sitting in the duck blind just having a great time. All of a sudden, he got real quiet. I waited a bit, and then he looked at me and asked: "Dad, do kids whose dads beat them at home see God differently than I do?" It was the start of probably the hardest and deepest questions he had ever asked in his life. And for the next three hours, we got the chance to talk about life and shoot at some ducks and geese. Neither of us will ever forget that trip.

As I've said previously: When I was growing up, my own dad didn't hunt or fish himself. But I can't express to you how much I learned about life when the two of us went out hunting and fishing *together*, with a campfire at the end of the day. That was when I truly began to understand the importance of doing things together. Dad never picked up a gun on any of these trips, and he rarely tried fishing. But he came along, and we talked a little bit